TERROR TUNNELS

ALSO BY ALAN DERSHOWITZ

TERROR TUNNELS

The Case for Israel's Just War Against Hamas

ALAN DERSHOWITZ

RosettaBooks®
NEW YORK: 2014

A GATESTONE PUBLICATION
INSTITUTE

This book is dedicated to all the innocent victims of Hamas's dead baby strategy—Palestinians and Israelis alike. It is also dedicated to the brave Israeli soldiers who gave their lives in an effort to protect these civilians.

CONTENTS

PART II
Operation Protective Edge

ACKNOWLEDGMENTS

This book was originally stimulated by my visit to a Hamas terror tunnel that was arranged by my dear friend and go-to guy in Israel, Danny Grossman. I was accompanied by two other dear friends, Tom Ashe and Dr. Michael Miller, who, along with their spouses, Joanne and Alisa, helped me develop this book. My wonderful wife, Carolyn, who also accompanied me to the tunnel, provided her usual support, encouragement, and insight. Our tunnel visit was enabled and personally guided by "R," a high ranking figure in the Israel Security Agency, which quietly fights for Israel's defense around the clock. I also acknowledge the assistance of Sarah Neely, Nicholas Maisel, Stella Frank, my son Elon, and the gang from "the porch."

TERROR TUNNELS

INTRODUCTION

ON JUNE 13, 2014, the commander of the southern region for the Israel Security Agency (ISA), together with the commander of the Gaza Division of the Israel Defense Forces (IDF), took me into a Hamas tunnel that had recently been discovered by a Bedouin tracker who serves in the IDF. The tunnel was a concrete bunker that extended several miles from its entrance in the Gaza Strip to its exit near an Israeli kibbutz kindergarten.

The tunnel had one purpose: to allow Hamas death squads to kill and kidnap Israelis. The commander told me that Israeli intelligence had identified more than two dozen additional tunnel entrances in the Gaza Strip. They had been identified by the large amounts of earth being removed to dig them. Although Israeli intelligence knew where these entrances were, they could not order an attack from the air, because they were built into civilian structures such as mosques, schools, hospitals, and private homes. Nor could Israel identify their underground routes from Gaza into Israel, or their intended exit points in Israel. Israeli scientists and military experts had spent millions of dollars in an effort to develop technologies that could find the underground routes and intended exits for tunnels that were as deep as a hundred feet beneath the earth, but they had not succeeded in finding a complete solution to this problem.[1] The planned exits from these tunnels in Israel were also a Hamas secret, hidden deep in the ground and incapable of being discovered by Israel until the Hamas fighters emerged. At that point it would be too late to prevent the death squads from doing their damage.

I was taken into the tunnel and saw the technological innovations: tracks on which small trains could transport kidnapped Israelis back to Gaza; telephone and electrical lines; crevices beneath schools and other civilian targets that could hold explosives; and smaller offshoot tunnels leading from the main tube to numerous exit points from which fighters could simultaneously emerge from different places.

As soon as I went down into the tunnel, I realized that Israel would have no choice but to take military action to destroy them. Israel had a technological response—though imperfect—to Hamas rockets. Its Iron Dome was capable of destroying approximately 85 percent of Hamas rockets fired at its population centers.[2] Moreover, it could attack rocket launchers from the air with sophisticated, GPS-guided bombs. But it had no complete technological answer to these terror tunnels. Subsequently, the media reported that Hamas may have been planning a Rosh Hashanah massacre during which hundreds of Hamas terrorists would simultaneously emerge from dozens of tunnels and slaughter hundreds, if not thousands, of Israeli civilians and soldiers.[3]

---

1 Recently, Israel announced that it was testing a new technology that could help locate the tunnel routes and exit points—see for example Inna Lazareva, "Israel Tests Hi-Tech Tunnel Detection System to Fight Threat from Underground," *The Telegraph* [Jaffa], 23 July 2014.

2 "Iron Dome: How Israel's Missile Defence System Works," *The Week*, 1 August 2014.

3 "Report: Hamas Planned Rosh Hashanah Attack through Gaza Tunnels," *JTA*, 28 July 2014, citing Maariv and "security sources."

If this report were true, as many in Israel believed it was, the Rosh Hashanah massacre would have been the equivalent of a hundred 9/11s in the United States. Even if it was an exaggeration, the tunnels certainly provided Hamas with the capability of wreaking havoc on Israeli citizens. There were other reports as well of planned attacks through the tunnels. As one resident of Sderot put it: "We used to look up to the sky in fear, but now we are looking down at the ground."[4]

To me, the only questions were *when* Israel would act, *how* it would act, *whether* it would be successful, and *what* the consequences would be. Could any nation tolerate this kind of threat to its citizens? Has any nation in history ever allowed tunnels to be dug under its border which would permit death squads to operate against its people?

I discussed these issues with Israeli prime minister Benjamin Netanyahu at a dinner in his home several days after my visit to the tunnel, and it became clear that the Israeli government had been concerned about the security threats posed by these terror tunnels ever since the tunnels were used to kidnap the young soldier Gilad Shalit and kill two of his compatriots.

Ironically, it was while we were in the tunnel that we learned that three Israeli high school students had been kidnapped. Their kidnapping, which Hamas subsequently acknowledged was done by its operatives, and their murder, was the beginning of what turned into Operation Protective Edge, which ended with the destruction of most of the tunnels. This book is about that operation and why Israel was justified—legally, morally, diplomatically, and politically—in responding to the dangers posed by the tunnels and the rocket attacks that preceded and followed their discovery.

4 Melanie Lidman, "They Thought it Was Rockets They Had to be Scared Of," *The Times of Israel*, 6 August 2014.

It is also about why so many in the media, academia, the international community, and the general public seem to blind themselves to the dangers posed by Hamas and blame Israel for actions *they would demand their own governments take*, were they faced with comparable threats.

Indeed, the United States is now leading a coalition of nations in an effort to destroy ISIS, employing many of the same military tactics for which some of these nations blamed Israel.

I believe that the "blame Israel" reaction has serious consequences, not only for Israel but for the people of Gaza, and for the democratic world in general. Blaming Israel only encourages Hamas to repeat its "dead baby strategy" and other terrorist groups to emulate it. This strategy, which has worked effectively, operates as follows: Hamas attacks Israel either by rockets or through tunnels, thereby forcing Israel to respond, as any democracy would do, to protect its citizens. Because Hamas fires its rockets and digs its tunnels from densely populated civilian areas, rather than from the many open areas of the Gaza Strip, the inevitable result is that a significant number of Palestinian civilians are killed. Hamas encourages this result, because it knows the media will focus more on the *photographs* of dead babies than on the *cause* of their death: namely, the decision by Hamas to use these babies and other civilians as human shields. Hamas quickly produces the dead babies to be shown around the world, while at the same time preventing the media from showing its rocket launchers and tunnels in densely populated areas. The world is outraged at the dead civilians and blames Israel for killing them. This only encourages Hamas to repeat its dead baby strategy following short cease-fires, during which they rearm and regroup.

In 2009, I published a short book entitled *The Case for Moral Clarity: Israel, Hamas and Gaza*. Very little has changed since that time, except that Hamas has built many more tunnels, and that the reach and sophistication of its rockets has increased.

I am writing this book to warn the world that unless Hamas's dead baby strategy is denounced and stopped—by the international community, the media, the academy, and good people of all religions, ethnicities, and nationalities—it will be coming "to a theater near you." Hamas repeatedly employs this despicable and unlawful strategy because it works! It works because despite the material losses Hamas suffers in its repeated military encounters with Israel, it always wins the public relations war, the legal war, the academic war, and the war for the naïve hearts, if not the wise minds, of young people. And if it is indeed winning these wars—if its dead baby strategy is working—why not repeat it every few years? That's why cease-fires between Israel and Hamas always mean that Israel "ceases" and Hamas "fires"—perhaps not immediately, while it regroups and rearms, but inevitably. And if it works for Hamas, why shouldn't other terrorist groups, like ISIS[5] and Boko Haram, adapt this strategy to their nefarious goals, as Hezbollah has already done?

The only way to end this cycle of death is to expose the Hamas dead baby strategy for what it is—a double war crime whose ultimate victims are civilian children, women, and men.

I have only one weapon in this war: my words. During the course of Operation Protective Edge I have tried to make the case for Israel's just war against Hamas's double war crime strategy. I have written more than two dozen op-eds, participated in several debates and television interviews, and

---

5 Different acronyms have been used to refer to the Islamic State of Iraq and Syria, or ISIS, including the Islamic State of Iraq and the Levant (ISIL) and simply the Islamic State (IS).

have spoken to numerous audiences. With this book, I seek to reach a larger audience and influence the most important tribunal in any democracy: the court of public opinion.

The book is divided into two parts. The first covers the run-up to the recent war in Gaza from the end of Operation Cast Lead (December 2008–January 2009) to just before the beginning of Operation Protective Edge (July–August 2014). The second deals with Operation Protective Edge and its aftermath.

My goal is to show that Israel's military actions in defense of its citizens have been just, and that they have been conducted in a just manner. They are no less just than the military actions being conducted by the United States and its allies against ISIS, al-Qaeda, and other terrorist groups. And they have been carried out at least as justly, with a lower percentage of civilian-to-combatant casualties.

Yet Israel has been unjustly condemned from too many corners, thus encouraging Hamas to continue its despicable and unlawful dead baby strategy. For the sake of justice and peace, the world must stop applying a double standard to the nation-state of the Jewish people.

Alan M. Dershowitz
New York, NY
September 2014

PART I

PRELUDE TO OPERATION PROTECTIVE EDGE

Operation Protective Edge—
The Historical Context

"**T**HOSE WHO DO NOT REMEMBER the past are condemned to repeat it." This truism, by philosopher George Santayana, well describes the current situation in the Middle East in general and Gaza in particular. Israelis and Palestinians have been condemned to repeat the tragedies of the past because history is neglected or misunderstood. That is why it is necessary to place the recent events in Gaza into a brief historical context.

On October 2, 2001, only three weeks after the terror attacks of September 11, President George W. Bush announced that the United States supported the creation of a Palestinian state. It was a major milestone for the Palestinian cause, since no previous American administration had officially acknowledged a Palestinian state as an explicit goal of US foreign policy. The announcement was all the more remarkable given that the US was still reeling in the wake of 9/11, and that Palestinian extremists were still using terror against Israelis to achieve their goals. The American announcement came just months after Yasser Arafat had rejected an offer of statehood by Israeli Prime Minister Ehud Barak and Bush's predecessor, Bill Clinton.[1]

Bush's announcement offered a unique opportunity to Palestinians to end the violence and begin building a new future. Hamas's response came a few weeks later, when it fired the first Qassam rocket at the Israeli town of Sderot, a city with a population of approximately 20,000, of which some two dozen were killed, hundreds wounded, and thousands traumatized. The Hamas website proudly proclaimed: "The Zionist army is afraid that the Palestinians will increase the range of the new rockets, placing the towns and villages in the [Zionist] entity in danger."[2] It was only the first of thousands of rockets that Hamas and other Palestinian terror organizations would fire in their relentless effort to kill Jews and destroy the peace process.

Rocket and mortar fire from the Gaza Strip peaked in late 2004 and early 2005. There was a brief halt in March 2005, in the aftermath of Mahmoud Abbas's victory in the Palestinian presidential elections, and an agreement signed by the various Palestinian factions in Cairo to halt violence. Hamas and other organizations merely used the lull to rearm, however. In August of that year, Israel carried out its disengagement from Gaza, voluntarily withdrawing thousands of settlers and soldiers, leaving twenty-one communities

---

1 This was neither the first nor last such offer. The Peel Commission in 1937, the UN in 1947, and Israel in 1967 made similar proposals, all of which were rejected by three noes: "no peace, no negotiation, no recognition." And in 2008, then–Prime Minister Ehud Olmert offered the Palestinians the most generous proposal, which they did not accept.

2 "Rocket Threat from the Gaza Strip, 2000–2007," Intelligence and Terrorism Information Center at the Israel Intelligence Heritage & Commemoration Center, citing the Hamas website following the first rocket fired at Sderot at the end of October 2001: 33–34.

behind and completely ending the Israeli presence there. The hope was that Palestinians would use the end of Israeli occupation to build Gaza's economy and prepare it for political independence, along with the West Bank, as part of a Palestinian state. Private donors stepped in to buy the Israeli greenhouses that had been left behind and hand them over to the Palestinian Authority. James Wolfenson, the former head of the World Bank, contributed $500,000 of his own money to the purchase. But almost immediately after the disengagement, Hamas and other terror organizations destroyed the greenhouses and renewed their rocket fire, launching a barrage of rockets at the Israeli towns of Sderot and Ashkelon. The immediate trigger was an accident during a Hamas victory rally, in which a truck filled with weapons exploded in a Gaza refugee camp, killing nineteen Palestinians. There was little media focus on, and no demonstrations against, these largely civilian deaths.

Rocket fire continued throughout the months that followed, though Israel was no longer occupying Gaza. In November 2005, Israel signed an agreement with the Palestinian Authority to open the Rafah Crossing on the Egypt-Gaza border. The agreement was part of an effort to encourage trade and economic development in Gaza, and to increase the responsibilities of the Palestinian government for the welfare of the Palestinian people. And, indeed, the Rafah Crossing remained open throughout the first half of 2006. The border remained open despite Hamas's victory in the Palestinian legislative elections in January 2006, which caused deep worry in Israel and throughout the international community. The Middle East Quartet—comprised of the European Union, United Nations, United States, and Russia—warned the new Palestinian government that further aid would be conditional on its "commitment to the principles of non-violence, recognition of Israel, and acceptance of previous agreements and obligations."[3] Hamas considered and rejected each of these conditions. That decision, in turn, prompted the Quartet, and Israel, to cut off financial assistance to the Palestinian Authority, though Israel continued to supply electricity and water to Gaza.

Hamas quickly resumed its attacks. In February alone, forty-seven rockets were fired. By June, Hamas and other groups had launched hundreds of Qassams, as well as an Iranian-made Grad rocket. On June 25, Hamas launched an attack inside Israel, having tunneled under the border near the Kerem Shalom (Vineyard of Peace) border crossing. In the ensuing battle, Hamas kidnapped an Israeli soldier named Gilad Shalit, killing two Israeli soldiers in the process and injuring others. Following the tunnel attack and kidnapping, Israel attacked terrorist targets in Gaza and closed the Rafah Crossing. The closure was not an attempt to punish Palestinians for the elections result five months before, but was the direct consequence of Hamas's attack on Israel.

Even after Hamas abducted Shalit, the Gaza borders were not completely closed. The Rafah Crossing was open for twenty-four days over the next six months, and some movement of people and goods—albeit restricted—was allowed. Throughout this time, rocket fire from the Gaza Strip continued to terrorize Israeli civilians. Still, the international community gave the Palestinian leaders another chance to meet the basic demands it had issued in January 2006. But the two main Palestinian factions—Fatah, which controlled the executive, and Hamas, which controlled the legislature—began fighting openly with each other. After extensive negotiations, the two parties agreed to form a unity government, which was formed in March 2007. But the rockets continued to rain down—reaching a record high

---

3 "Quartet Statement - 30 January 2006," Middle East Quartet, London, http://www.quartetrep.org/quartet/pages/the-quartet/.

of 257 in May 2007—and in June 2007, Hamas launched a military coup against the Fatah executive, driving its leaders out of Gaza and killing over one hundred of their fellow Palestinians, including many civilians. Again, the events garnered little media focus and no protest marches. With the entire territory of Gaza under its iron-fisted control, Hamas increased rocket attacks against Israel, with other Palestinian terror organizations joining in. These attacks accelerated dramatically after Israel and the exiled Palestinian Authority leaders—still legally governed by Fatah, in the eyes of the international community—signed an agreement in Annapolis, Maryland, in November 2007, pledging to work toward a two-state solution.

It was only after Hamas's coup, and the heavy rocket attacks that followed, that Israel imposed more extensive sanctions on Gaza. In January 2008—two years after Hamas took power, and after thousands of rockets and mortars had fallen on Israel's southern towns—Israel began restricting fuel and electricity to Gaza, in accordance with a nuanced ruling by Israel's High Court of Justice. Still, it continued to allow fuel and humanitarian aid to enter, and allowed Palestinians to come in to Israel to receive medical treatment in Israeli hospitals. Israel did not want ordinary Palestinians to suffer and did all that it could to alleviate their living conditions while reducing Hamas's ability to function as a terrorist regime. And yet Hamas continued to smuggle weapons into Gaza via underground tunnels on the Egyptian border. More than two thousand rockets and mortars were launched from Gaza into Israel in the first six months of 2008. In June of 2008, presidential candidate Barak Obama visited Sderot, and after viewing the rocket residues and meeting with residents, this is what he said:

> I don't think any country would find it acceptable to
> have missiles raining down on the heads of their citizens.

The first job of any nation state is to protect its citizens. And so I can assure you that if—I don't even care if I was a politician. If somebody was sending rockets into my house where my two daughters sleep at night, I'm going to do everything in my power to stop that. And I would expect Israelis to do the same.

In December 2008, Hamas unilaterally declared that it would resume its attacks with full force—and it promptly did so, forcing Israel to respond with Operation Cast Lead in late December of 2008.

When these facts are examined, it is clear that Palestinian rocket attacks against Israeli civilians were not a response to Gaza's increasing isolation, but the cause. The first rocket attacks began in October 2001, precisely when the world was most eager to create a viable Palestinian state. They continued even after Israel pulled its army and its settlements out of Gaza in 2005. They accelerated after Hamas took power in 2006, increasing dramatically in 2007 when Israel and the Palestinian Authority resolved to renew negotiations toward a two-state solution. And the attacks were renewed in December 2008 when Hamas unilaterally declared that it would refuse to extend a period of calm that had been accepted by both sides.

The sanctions that were imposed on Gaza—not only by Israel, but the world—were the direct result of Hamas's refusal to meet the international community's basic, reasonable demands: stop terror, recognize Israel, and respect previous agreements. Even after Hamas took power in the 2006 elections, the Gaza borders remained relatively open, until Hamas escalated the conflict by abducting Gilad Shalit in June 2006, overthrowing the legitimate Palestinian executive in a violent coup in June 2007, and launching more and more rockets and mortars at Israeli civilians. Hamas brought about the isolation of Gaza because it is neither interested in peace nor in the welfare of the Palestinian people. Instead, it is fanatically committed to the destruction of Israel itself, a goal it pursues using weapons and funding it receives from the Islamic Republic of Iran, for which Hamas acts as a proxy and whose ambitions of regional domination it serves. More recently, Hamas has also been supported by Qatar and Turkey.

Israelis and Palestinians have the same right to live in peace. Hamas and its fellow terror organizations deny that right, and disrupt every attempt to move the peace process forward. That is why Operation Cast Lead, which ended on January 21, 2009, was necessary.

It was against this backdrop that I began to write a series of op-eds during Operation Cast Lead. These op-eds comprised the bulk of my short book, *The Case For Moral Clarity: Israel, Hamas and Gaza.* Following the publication of that book, the *Goldstone Report* was issued under the auspices of a UN fact-finding mission. It accused Israel of war crimes during Operation Cast Lead and exculpated Hamas from the charge that it used civilians as human shields. It turned a military defeat suffered by Hamas into a legal and public relations victory. Because of its importance, I begin this book with my response to that mendacious screed. The *Goldstone Report* not only falsified the past; it had a negative influence on the future by encouraging Hamas to repeat its own double war crimes: firing rockets at Israeli civilians *from behind* Palestinian human shields—and killing and kidnapping Israeli civilians and soldiers through its terrorist tunnels.

2

The Case Against
the *Goldstone Report*—
and Why It Still Matters

January 27, 2010

T HE GOLDSTONE REPORT is much more scurrilous than most of its detractors (and supporters) believe. According to the report, Israel used the more than 8,000 rocket attacks on its civilians merely as a pretext, an excuse, a cover for the real purpose of Operation Cast Lead, which was to target innocent Palestinian civilians—children, women, the elderly—for death. This criminal objective was explicitly decided upon by the highest levels of the Israeli government and military, and constitutes a deliberate and willful war crime. The report found these serious charges "to be firmly based in fact" and had "no doubt" of their truth.

In contrast, the United Nations Fact Finding Mission on the Gaza Conflict decided that Hamas was not guilty of deliberately and willfully using the civilian population as human shields. It found "no evidence" that Hamas fighters "engaged in combat in civilian dress," "no evidence" that "Palestinian combatants mingled with the civilian population with the intention of shielding themselves from attack," and no support for the claim that mosques were used to store weapons.

The report is demonstrably wrong about both of these critical conclusions. The hard evidence conclusively proves that the exact opposite is true, namely that: 1) Israel did not have a policy of targeting innocent civilians for death. Indeed the IDF went to unprecedented lengths to minimize civilian casualties; and 2) that Hamas did have a deliberate policy of having its combatants dress in civilian clothing, fire their rockets from densely populated areas, use civilians as human shields, and store weapons in mosques.[1]

What is even more telling than its erroneous conclusions, however, is its deliberately skewed methodology, particularly the manner in which it used and evaluated similar evidence very differently, depending on whether it favored the Hamas or Israeli side.

I have written a detailed analysis of the Goldstone methodology, which is now available online.[2] It is being sent to the Secretary General of the United Nations for inclusion in critiques of the *Goldstone Report* received by the United Nations. This analysis documents the distortions, misuses of evidence, and bias of the report and those who wrote it. It demonstrates that the evidence relied on by the report, as well as the publicly available evidence it deliberately chose to ignore, disproves its own conclusions.

1 See for example: Steven Erlanger, "A Gaza War Full of Traps and Trickery," the *New York Times*, 10 January 2009; Yaakov Katz, "Hamas Used Almost 100 Mosques for Military Purposes," *The Jerusalem Post*, 15 March 2010; and "Evidence of the Use of the Civilian Population as Human Shields," Intelligence and Terrorism Information Center at the Israel Intelligence Heritage and Commemoration Center (IICC), 4 February 2009.

2 Alan Dershowitz, "The Case Against the *Goldstone Report*: A Study in Evidentiary Bias," Harvard Law School, 27 January 2010.

The central issue that distinguishes the conclusions the *Goldstone Report* reached regarding Israel, on the one hand, and Hamas, on the other, is intentionality. The report finds that the most serious accusation against Israel, namely the killing of civilians, was intentional and deliberately planned at the highest levels. The report also finds that the most serious accusations made against Hamas, namely that their combatants wore civilian clothing to shield themselves from attack, mingled among the civilian populations, and used civilians as human shields, was unintentional. These issues are, of course, closely related.

If it were to turn out that there was no evidence that Hamas ever operated from civilian areas, and that the IDF knew this, then the allegation that the IDF, by firing into civilian areas, deliberately intended to kill Palestinian civilians, would be strengthened. But if it were to turn out that the IDF reasonably believed that Hamas fighters were deliberately using civilians as shields, then this fact would weaken the claim that the IDF had no military purpose in firing into civilian areas. Moreover, if Hamas did use human shields, then the deaths of Palestinian civilians would be more justly attributable to Hamas than to Israel.

Since intentionality, or lack thereof, was so important to the report's conclusions, it would seem essential that the report would apply the same evidentiary standards, rules, and criteria in determining the intent of Israel and in determining the intent of Hamas.

Yet a careful review of the report makes it crystal clear that its writers applied totally different standards, rules, and criteria in evaluating the intent of the parties to the conflict. The report resolved all doubts against Israel in concluding that its leaders intended to kill civilians, while resolving all doubts in favor of Hamas in concluding that it did not intend to use Palestinian civilians as human shields.

Moreover, when it had precisely the same sort of evidence in relation to both sides—for example, statements by leaders prior to the commencement of the operation—it attributed significant weight to the Israeli statements, while entirely discounting comparable Hamas statements. This sort of evidentiary bias, though subtle, permeates the entire report.

In addition to the statements of leaders, which are treated so differently, the report takes a completely different view regarding the inferring of intent from action. When it comes to Israel, the report repeatedly looks to results and infers from the results that they must have been intended. But when it comes to Hamas, it refuses to draw inferences regarding intent from results.

For example, it acknowledges that some combatants wore civilian clothes, and it offers no reasonable explanation for why this would be so other than to mingle indistinguishably among civilians. Yet it refuses to infer intent from these actions. Highly relevant to the report's conclusion that militants did not intend for their actions to shield themselves from counterattack is that the mission was "unable to make any determination on the general allegation that Palestinian armed groups used mosques for military purpose," "did not find any evidence to support the allegations that hospital facilities were used by the Gaza authorities or by Palestinian armed groups to shield military activities," did not find evidence "that ambulances were used to transport combatants or for other military purposes," and did not find "that Palestinian armed groups engaged in combat activities from United Nations facilities that were used as shelters during the military operations."

There is, however, hard evidence that Hamas did operate in mosques and, at the very least, near hospitals. Circumstantial evidence (precise weaponry) was used to prove Israeli intent. Regarding Hamas, the circumstantial evidence is even stronger in inferring intent. It is beyond obvious that militants do not fire rockets in the vicinity of mosques or hospitals because it is easier to launch rockets near community institutions. Rather, they do so only because of the special protections afforded to hospitals and religious centers in war.

The report—commissioned by an organization with a long history of anti-Israel bigotry, and written by biased "experts," with limited experience—is one-sided and wrong in its fundamental conclusions. This should not be surprising since conclusions can be no better than the methodology employed, and the methodology employed in this report is fundamentally flawed.

So now it is up to Richard Goldstone to explain the evidentiary bias that is so obviously reflected in the report, and that is documented in my lengthier analysis available online. The burden is on him to justify the very different methodologies used in the report to arrive at its conclusions regarding the intentions of Israel and the intentions of Hamas. Failure to assume that burden will constitute an implicit admission that the conclusions reached in the *Goldstone Report* are not worthy of consideration by people of good will.

3

Finally, A Hamas Leader Admits that Israel Killed Mostly Combatants in Gaza

December 17, 2010

SINCE THE END of the Gaza War in January 2009, Israel has stood accused of targeting civilians rather than terrorist combatants. The Israeli Defense Force has claimed that during Operation Cast Lead it targeted only combatants in its efforts to protect its civilians from rocket attacks. It has also claimed that most of the dead were combatants and issued lists of names of many of the combatants killed and identified them as members of the specific Hamas military units. Despite unprecedented efforts to avoid civilian casualties—including hundreds of thousands of leaflets, telephone calls, and nonlethal, noise-making warning bombs[1]—some civilians were killed, because

---

1 "IDF Phones Gaza Residents to Warn Them of Imminent Strikes," *Haaretz*, 2 January 2009. See also: Adam Taylor, "'Roof Knocking': The Israeli Military's Tactic of Phoning Palestinians it is about to Bomb," *The Washington Post*, 9 July 2014.

Hamas deliberately hid behind civilians, using them as shields, when they fired rockets at Israeli civilians.

Following the end of the Gaza War, which temporarily stopped Hamas rocket attacks against Israeli civilians, there was a great debate about the number of Gaza civilians actually killed, and the ratio of civilian to combatant deaths during this difficult military operation.

The Israel Defense Force put the total number of known combatants killed at 709 and the number of known civilian deaths at 295, with 162 (mostly men of fighting age) "unknown."[2] Such a ratio, if true, would be far better than that achieved by any other nation in a comparable conflict. Not surprisingly, Israel's enemies initially disputed this ratio and claimed that the number of combatants killed was far lower and the number of civilians far higher. The United Nations, the *Goldstone Report*, various human rights organizations, and many in the media automatically rejected Israel's documented figures, preferring the distorted numbers offered by Hamas and other Palestinian sources.

But a statement recently made by a Hamas leader confirms that Israel was correct in claiming that approximately 700 combatants were killed.

First, a word about the context of the Hamas statement. In the aftermath of the war, Hamas has come under considerable criticism from rival terrorist groups for not doing enough to defend Gaza and for allowing so many civilian casualties. So, in a recent interview with a London paper, Al-Hayat, Fathi Hamad, Hamas's Interior Minister, responded to these criticisms as follows:

> It has been said that the people were harmed by the war, but is Hamas not part of the people? It is a fact that on

2 Yaakov Lappin, "IDF Releases Cast Lead Casualty Numbers," *The Jerusalem Post*, 1 January 2010.

the first day of the war Israel struck police headquarters and killed 250 members of Hamas and the various factions, in addition to the 200–300 operatives from the [Izz al-Din] al-Qassam Brigades. In addition, 150 security personnel were killed, and the rest were from people.[3]

This statement not only supports the Israeli numbers, but it also acknowledges what Israel has long said about the 250 policemen who were killed on the first day of combat: they were "members of Hamas and the various factions" and were indeed combatants by any realistic definition of that term.

Fathi Hamad's figures are in striking contrast to those originally issued by Palestinian groups, which claimed that only forty-eight combatants were killed and that the total amounted to a mere 17 percent of all fatalities.

Because it uncritically accepted the original Hamas claims of very few combatant deaths, the *Goldstone Report* was able to reach its flawed conclusion that the *purpose* of the operation must have been to kill civilians, not combatants. This is what the *Goldstone Report* said:

> The Mission notes that the statistics from non-governmental sources are generally consistent. Statistics alleging that fewer than one out of five persons killed in an armed conflict was a combatant... raise very serious concerns about the way Israel conducted the military operations in Gaza. The counterclaims published by the Government of Israel fall short of international law standards.

3 The original text of the interview in Arabic, as reprinted in the Hamas newspaper *Felesteen,* can be found on the website of the Meir Amit Intelligence and Terrorism Information Center. It was also reported by *Agence France Presse.*

Now that the truth has been admitted by the Hamas leadership—that as many as seven hundred combatants were, in fact, killed—the Goldstone Commission is obliged to reconsider its false conclusion and correct its deeply flawed report.

Richard Goldstone himself has repeatedly said that he hoped that new evidence will prove his conclusions wrong. Well, this new evidence—a classic admission against interest—does just that!

The original false figures have also been submitted by the Palestinian Authority to the International Criminal Court. It too has an obligation to correct the record. It would be an outrageous miscarriage of justice for the International Criminal Court to open an investigation of a nation that, in actuality, had the *best* ratio of combatant to civilian deaths in any comparable war.

The admission by Fathi Hamad that Israel's figures were correct and those originally offered by Palestinian groups were false exposes the rush to judgment against Israel that has stained the so-called human rights community so often in the past. It is essential that this new evidence be widely circulated, which it has not been to date, and that those who condemned Israel on the basis of false allegations correct the record. Don't hold your breath! In today's distorted world of human rights, truth takes a backseat to ideology, and false claims—especially those that support radical ideologies—persist even after they have been exposed.

4

Goldstone Needs to Recant in Light of the New Evidence

January 11, 2011

C AN RICHARD GOLDSTONE'S tarnished reputation be rehabilitated without him acknowledging that the evidence, including new information, proves he was wrong? There is a politically motivated effort under way to rehabilitate the tarnished reputation of Richard Goldstone. His reputation suffered not only from his association with the discredited *Goldstone Report* regarding the war in Gaza, but also from recent revelations of the ignoble role he played as a hanging and torturing judge while serving the apartheid regime in South Africa.

For strident enemies of Israel, such as the hard left *Nation* magazine, Goldstone was a hero. They couldn't care less that the "findings" of the *Goldstone Report* were contradicted by the physical evidence, including video and audiotapes. They ignored the fact that a leading Hamas figure acknowledged that most of those killed by Israeli fire were combatants, including police officers trained to fight against Israel. They couldn't be bothered by the disclosure that their hero had ordered the torture of black prisoners and the execution of black defendants who never would have been subject to whipping or capital punishment had they been white. "He was just doing his job," his defenders claimed, an excuse reminiscent of even darker times. The *Nation*, and others who toe to their "Israel is always wrong" line, cared only that Goldstone, a Jew and a Zionist to boot, had concluded that it was Israeli policy—determined at the highest level—to target Palestinian civilians, and that it was not Hamas policy to fire their rockets at Israeli civilians while hiding among Palestinian civilians and using them as human shields.

Almost no reasonable observers, who are knowledgeable of Israeli and Hamas policies and actions, credit these conclusions. Even Israel's most strident internal critics—and there are many, and they are quite vocal—disbelieve these extreme exaggerations.

The only reason the *Goldstone Report* has been given any credibility by anyone is because Goldstone himself is Jewish and purports to be a Zionist. Indeed those seeking to rehabilitate his reputation constantly point to his Jewish background.

Consider a recent article by Letty Pogrebin in the *Forward*,[1] which appears to be an opening salvo in the battle to rehabilitate Goldstone. It is part of a forthcoming book being published by—you guessed it—The Nation Press. She argues that Israeli efforts to "bury" the report have been "complicated" from the start by "an inconvenient truth: Goldstone was one of them—a Jew, and not just any Jew, an exemplary one." But the fact that Goldstone is a Jew is not simply a passive "truth." Instead the decision to hire Goldstone precisely because he is a Jew was a critical tactical decision made by the United Nations Human Rights

---

1 Letty C. Pogrebin, "The Un-Jewish Assault on Richard Goldstone," *The Jewish Daily Forward*, 29 December 2010.

Council, whose long history of applying a double standard to Israel has denied it any credibility.

Pogrebin's defense of Richard Goldstone is as factually inaccurate as the *Goldstone Report* itself. Pogrebin's thesis can be summarized in her own words, "Rather than discuss the contents of the report—which concluded that during the 2008–2009 Gaza War, Israel, as well as Hamas, may have committed war crimes—Israel's defenders launched an all-points campaign to bury it." She claims that "almost no one is talking about his findings." She is dead wrong. Within days of the report's publication, there were numerous discussions of the contents and findings of the report. I myself published a forty-nine-page point-by-point specific criticism of the report's contents entitled "The Case against the *Goldstone Report*: A Study in Evidentiary Bias."[2] In it I focused on the report's main findings that 1) the Israeli government had a policy of targeting civilians; and 2) that Hamas did not have a policy of hiding behind civilians. I proved that both these findings were contradicted by the evidence. Goldstone has never responded to my substantive criticism.

The Israeli government issued very specific point-by-point rebuttals of Goldstone's findings, to which he has never responded. Moreover, when students at the Fordham Law School invited Goldstone and me to discuss the contents of the report, Goldstone declined, even though he was teaching at Fordham at the time. I accepted and presented a specific response to the contents of the report. Most recently, I wrote an op-ed showing that an important Hamas leader had made admissions undercutting the report's findings.[3]

2 Alan Dershowitz, "The Case Against the *Goldstone Report*: A Study in Evidentiary Bias," Harvard Law School, 27 January 2010.

3 Alan Dershowitz, "Finally, a Hamas Leader Admits that Israel Killed Mostly Combatants in Gaza," *The World Post*, 17 December 2010.

Again, no response from Goldstone. So Pogrebin simply makes it up when she says that Israel's defenders refuse to "discuss the contents of the report."

Richard Goldstone can be rehabilitated *only* if he comes forward and acknowledges that the totality of the evidence—including the recent admissions of the Hamas leader—demonstrates that the central conclusions of the *Goldstone Report* were wrong. Goldstone has said that he hopes that new evidence proves them wrong. Now is the time for him to show whether he is mensch enough to step forward and set the record straight. So far he has been silent. The world is waiting to hear what he has to say.

5

How Goldstone Is Making Peace
More Difficult

January 9, 2010

WHENEVER EFFORTS ARE MADE to bring about a peaceful resolution of the Israeli-Palestinian conflict, the eight-hundred-pound gorilla in the room is Richard Goldstone. His notorious report sends the following message to the Israeli government: If you end your military occupation of the West Bank, and the Palestinians use their new territory to launch rockets and other attacks against Israel, you will not be able to defend yourself without Goldstone and his colleagues condemning you for taking actions in self-defense.

This is a realistic threat, as evidenced by what happened after Israel ended its military occupation of the Gaza Strip. Hamas took over by military force and used the newly liberated lands not to build a civil society but to attack Israel. They fired hundreds of rockets at Israeli civilians and made life impossible for nearly a million Israelis living in the south of Israel. After enduring these rockets for years, and futilely seeking help from the international community, Israel did what any democracy would do: they defended their civilians against the war crimes being perpetrated by Hamas. But Hamas poses a difficult military target since it deliberately hides its fighters among civilians and fires its rockets from schoolyards, hospitals, and mosques. Considering these difficulties, Israel did a commendable job at stopping most of the rockets while minimizing civilian casualties.

Nonetheless, Richard Goldstone issued a blood libel against Israel, accusing its leaders of deliberately setting out to maximize civilian deaths. It also exculpated Hamas from the war crime of using civilians as human shields. The Palestinian Authority—yes, the Palestinian Authority, not Hamas—filed formal charges against Israel in the International Criminal Court. This, despite the fact that President Abbas and his subordinates urged Israel to be even more aggressive against Hamas in Gaza so that the Palestinian Authority could regain its lawful power. Enemies of Israel throughout the world have used the notorious *Goldstone Report* in an effort to delegitimize the Jewish state.

When I was recently in Israel for a month, I spoke to all of its political and military leaders. The *Goldstone Report* was very much on their minds as they contemplated the possibility of withdrawal from the West Bank. I also discussed the *Goldstone Report* with Palestinian Prime Minister Salam Fayyad, who acknowledged to me that by demanding that criminal charges be brought against Israel in the International Criminal Court he was simply "playing a card." Well, if there is to be an end of Israel's occupation of the West Bank, the Palestinian Authority will have to stop playing the delegitimation card. It will have to work together with Israel to prevent a repeat in the West Bank of what happened in Gaza. The recent claim of responsibility by Hamas for the murder of four Israelis in the West Bank does not bode well for the peace process. It demonstrates that the Palestinian

Authority has only limited control over Hamas, and that Hamas can play its "violence card" any time it chooses.

For the peace process to have any chance of success, the international community must categorically reject the *Goldstone Report* and what it represents. It must reaffirm Israel's right to defend itself against attacks from territory it cedes to the Palestinians. To its credit, the Obama administration has rejected the *Goldstone Report*, but it must go even further. It must assure Israel—publically and unequivocally—that it will vigorously defend Israel's right to protect its civilians from rocket attacks, suicide bombings, and roadside shootings.

Barak Obama's statement when he visited Sderot—that he "would expect Israel to do" everything in its power to stop the rocket attacks—must become a firm basis of American policy, if and when Israel leaves the West Bank.

So, thank you Richard Goldstone for making peace more difficult. There are some who are proposing Goldstone for a Nobel Peace Prize. Were he to win it, he would be in the company of Yasser Arafat, who also won the prize, before he rejected the Clinton/Barak offer that would have created a Palestinian state, with its capital in Jerusalem and with a $35 billion reparation package for the so-called refugees. Prince Bandar of Saudi Arabia was more prescient than the Nobel committee when he accused Arafat of committing a crime against peace and warning him that he was rejecting the best offer the Palestinians would ever get. Both Goldstone and Arafat deserve a prize, but it should be awarded by Hamas and Ahmadinejad rather than by the Nobel committee.

Let us hope that the barriers to peace erected by Richard Goldstone and Yasser Arafat can be overcome at the ongoing meetings convened by the Obama Administration. It won't be easy.

AUTHOR'S NOTE:

On April 1, 2011, Richard Goldstone wrote an op-ed in the Washington Post in which he admitted that "if I had known then what I know now, the *Goldstone Report* would have been a different document." In particular, he backed away from allegations that Israel had committed war crimes and crimes against humanity by intentionally targeting civilians.[1] He also explicitly recognized the long-standing anti-Israel bias of the UN Human Rights Council. Unfortunately, but perhaps unsurprisingly, the other members of the Goldstone Commission refused to reconsider their conclusions, even in light of the new evidence. Accordingly, the report retains its status as the official conclusion of the United Nations Council on Human Rights, despite its demonstrable factual falsity and the rejection of its most important conclusions by its chairman.

---

[1] Richard Goldstone, "Reconsidering the *Goldstone Report* on Israel and War Crimes," *The Washington Post*, 1 April 2011.

6

The Phony War Crimes
Accusation Against Israel

January 26, 2009

EVERY TIME ISRAEL SEEKS TO DEFEND its civilians against terrorist attacks, it is accused of war crimes by various United Nations agencies, hard left academics, and some in the media. It is a totally phony charge concocted as part of Hamas's strategy—supported by many on the hard left—to delegitimate and demonize the Jewish state. Israel is the only democracy in the world ever accused of war crimes when it fights a defensive war to protect its civilians. This is remarkable, especially in light of the fact that Israel has killed far fewer civilians than any other country in the world that has faced comparable threats. In the most recent war in Gaza, fewer than a thousand civilians—even by Hamas's skewed count—have been killed. This, despite the fact that no one can now deny that Hamas had employed a deliberate policy of using children, schools, mosques, apartment buildings, and other civilian areas as shields from behind which to launch its deadly antipersonnel rockets. The Israeli Air Force has produced unchallengeable video evidence of this Hamas war crime.

Just to take one comparison, consider the recent wars waged by Russia against Chechnya. In these wars, Russian troops have killed tens of thousands of Chechen civilians, some of them willfully, at close range and in cold blood. Yet those radical academics who scream bloody murder against Israel (particularly in England) have never called for war crime tribunals to be convened against Russia. Nor have they called for war crimes charges to be filed against any other of the many countries that routinely kill civilians, not in an effort to stop enemy terrorists, but just because it is part of their policy.

Nor did we see the Nuremberg-type rallies that were directed against Israel when hundreds of thousands of civilians were being murdered in Rwanda, in Darfur, and in other parts of the world. These bigoted hate-fests are reserved for Israel.

The accusation of war crimes is nothing more than a tactic selectively invoked by Israel's enemies. Those who cry "war crime" against Israel don't generally care about war crimes, as such; indeed, they often support them when engaged in by countries they like. What these people care about, and all they seem to care about, is Israel. Whatever Israel does is wrong regardless of the fact that so many other countries do worse.

When I raised this concern in a recent debate, my opponent accused me of changing the subject. He said we were talking about Israel, not Chechnya or Darfur. This reminded me of a famous exchange between Harvard's racist president, Abbott Lawrence Lowell, and the great American judge Learned Hand. Lowell announced that he wanted to reduce the number of Jews at Harvard, because "Jews cheat." Judge Hand replied that "Christians also cheat." Lowell responded, "You're changing the subject. We are talking about Jews."

Well, you can't just talk about Jews. Nor can you just talk about the nation-state of the Jewish people. Any discussion of war crimes must be comparative and contextual. If Russia did not commit war crimes when its soldiers massacred tens of thousands of Chechens (not even in a defensive war), then on what basis could Israel be accused of accidentally killing a far fewer number of human shields in an effort to protect its civilians? What are the standards? Why are they not being applied equally? Can human rights endure in the face of such unequal and selective application? These are the questions the international community should be debating, not whether Israel, and Israel alone, violated the norms of that vaguest of notions called "international law" or the "law of war."

If Israel, and Israel alone among democracies fighting defensive wars, were ever to be charged with war crimes, that would mark the end of international human rights law as a neutral arbitrator of conduct. Any international tribunal that were to charge Israel, having not charged the many nations that have done far worse, will lose any remaining legitimacy among fair-minded people of good will.

If the laws of war in particular, and international human rights in general, are to endure, they must be applied to nations in order of the seriousness of the violations, not in order of the political unpopularity of the nations. The worst must be charged first. If the law of war were applied in this manner, Israel would be among the last, and certainly not the first, charged.

7

The Case Against "Universal Jurisdiction"

October 6, 2009

I N SEPTEMBER OF 2009, Israeli Defense Minister Ehud Barak—the former dovish prime minister who offered the Palestinians a state on all of the Gaza Strip, 95 percent of the West Bank, and a capital in East Jerusalem—was arrested when he set foot in Great Britain. (He was quickly released on grounds of diplomatic immunity because he was an official visitor.)[1] After that, Moshe Yaalon, an Israeli government minister and former army chief of staff, was forced to cancel a trip he was scheduled to make in London on behalf of a charity, for fear that he too would be arrested.

The charges against these two distinguished public officials are that they committed war crimes against Palestinian terrorists and civilians. Yaalon was accused in connection with the 2002 targeted killing of Salah Shehadeh, a notorious terrorist who was responsible for the deaths of hundreds of Israeli civilians and was planning the murders of hundreds more. As a result of faulty intelligence, the rocket

1 Ian Black and Ian Cobain, "Israeli Minister Ehud Barak faces War Crimes Arrest Threat During UK Visit," *The Guardian*, 29 September 2009.

that killed Shehadeh also killed several civilians who were nearby, including members of his family. Barak is being accused of war crimes in connection with Israel's recent military effort to stop rockets from being fired at its civilians from the Gaza Strip.

The British government and British prosecutors have not supported the arrests of Barak and Yaalon. Those demanding the arrest of these Israelis are hard-left political activists who are seeking to invoke so-called "universal jurisdiction" against those whom they consider guilty of war crimes and genocide. They have absolutely zero interest in human rights, in the laws of war, or in preventing genocide. Indeed, many of them supported the Cambodian genocide and have refused to condemn the Rwanda and Darfur genocides. They would never dream of demanding the arrest of Hamas murderers who target Israeli schoolchildren for suicide bombings or rocket attacks. They are willfully misusing these concepts—human rights, universal jurisdiction—to serve their anti-Israel and anti-Western ideology. What they are doing undercuts the neutrality and value of these protections.

If they were at all interested in human rights, they would be going after the worst first—those who murder innocent civilians as part of a campaign of ethnic cleansing or genocide. But they are interested in Israel and Israel alone. That's why they demand boycotts and divestment only from the Jewish state and not from real human rights violators. Indeed, most of them would fervently reject sanctions against Iran, North Korea, Libya, Venezuela, China, Zimbabwe, Syria, or Saudi Arabia.

It is disgraceful that Israeli leaders cannot walk the streets of London safely, while Hamas and Hezbollah leaders are honored and celebrated. The time has come for Israel to confront this issue directly and to take legal action to prevent radical Israel-haters from misusing decent laws to achieve indecent results. Just imagine what a trial would look like if it were conducted fairly and objectively. The Israelis would be able to prove that their campaign of targeted assassinations of terrorists has worked effectively to reduce terrorism against Israeli citizens and others. Israel has inadvertently killed some civilians but thanks in particular to the hard work of Air Force chief Elizer Shkedi, the ratio of civilians to combatants killed has improved dramatically from a "1:1 ratio between killed terrorists and civilians in 2003 to a 1:28 ratio in late 2005."[2] Indeed, the current ratio is at its lowest ever at more than 1:30.

This is the best ratio of any country in the world that is fighting asymmetrical warfare against terrorists who hide behind civilians. It is far better than the ratio achieved by Great Britain and the United States in Iraq or Afghanistan, where both nations employ targeted killings of terrorist leaders. Recall that it was Great Britain that implemented a policy during the Second World War of targeting civilians in cities such as Dresden and that it was the United States that implemented the same policy in its firebombing of Tokyo. Indeed, it is fair to say that no country in modern history has ever been more protective of enemy civilians than Israel has been during its seventy-five-year fight against terrorism.

As British military expert Colonel Richard Kemp put it during Operation Cast Lead:

> [f]rom my knowledge of the IDF and from the extent to which I have been following the current operation, I don't think there has ever been a time in the history of warfare when any army has made more efforts to reduce

2 Amos Harel, "Pinpoint Attacks on Gaza More Precise," *Haaretz*, 30 December 2007. These figures are for targeted killings, not for wartime attacks against rockets and tunnels in densely populated areas.

civilian casualties and deaths of innocent people than the IDF is doing today in Gaza.

> ...Hamas, the enemy they have been fighting, has been trained extensively by Iran and by Hezbollah, to fight among the people, to use the civilian population in Gaza as a human shield... Hamas factor in the uses of the population as a major part of their defensive plan. So even though as I say, Israel, the IDF, has taken enormous steps... to reduce civilian casualties, it is impossible, it is impossible to stop that happening when the enemy has been using civilians as human shields.

Recall that before Israel went into the Gaza Strip, nearly ten thousand rockets had been fired at its civilians from behind human shields. No nation is obliged, under international law, to accept the risks of catastrophic outcomes from these antipersonnel rockets.

So let there be a legal proceeding—a fair one in an objective forum—in which Israel's policies are tested against those of other countries. The end result would be that Ehud Barak and Moshe Yaalon will be able to hold their heads up high and walk through the streets of any Western city in the full knowledge that what they have done meets and indeed exceeds every standard of international law applicable to their conduct.

8

If Israel Killed Mahmoud al-Mabhouh, Did It Have the Right To?

February 18, 2010

I DON'T KNOW whether Israel did or did not assassinate the leader of the Hamas military wing, Mahmoud al-Mabhouh. But assuming for argument's sake that the Mossad made the hit, did it have the right to engage in this "extrajudicial assassination?"

Not all extrajudicial killings are unlawful. Every soldier who kills an enemy combatant engages in an extrajudicial killing, as does every policeman who shoots a fleeing felon. There are several complex legal questions involved in assessing these situations.

First, was the person who was killed a combatant in relation to those who killed him? If Israel killed Mabhouh, there can be absolutely no doubt that he was a combatant. He was actively participating in an ongoing war by Hamas against Israeli civilians. Indeed, it is likely that he was killed while on a military mission to Iran in order to secure unlawful antipersonnel rockets that target Israeli civilians. Both the United States and Great Britain routinely killed such combatants during the Second World War, whether they were in uniform or not. Moreover, Hamas combatants deliberately remove their uniforms while engaged in combat.

So if the Israeli Air Force had killed Mabhouh while he was in Gaza, there would be absolutely no doubt that their action would be lawful. It does not violate international law to kill a combatant, regardless of where the combatant is found, whether he is awake or asleep and whether or not he is engaged in active combat at the moment of his demise.

But Mabhouh was not killed in Gaza. He was killed in Dubai. It is against the law of Dubai for an Israeli agent to kill a combatant against Israel while he is in Dubai. So the people who engaged in the killing presumptively violated the domestic law of Dubai, unless there is a defense to such a killing based on international principles regarding enemy combatants. It is unlikely that any defense would be available to an Israeli or someone working on behalf of Israel, since Dubai does not recognize Israel's right to kill enemy combatants on its territory.

If it could be proved that Israel was responsible for the hit—an extremely unlikely situation—then only Dubai could lawfully bring Israelis to trial. They would not be properly subjected to prosecution before an international tribunal. But what if a suspect was arrested in England, the United States, or some other Western country and Dubai sought his extradition? That would pose an interesting legal, diplomatic, political, and moral dilemma. Traditional extradition treaties do not explicitly cover situations of this kind. This was not an ordinary murder. It was carried out as a matter of state policy as part of an ongoing war. A Western democracy would certainly have the right and the power to refuse to extradite. But they might decide, for political or diplomatic reasons, to turn the person over to Dubai.

Turning now to the moral considerations that might influence a decision whether to extradite, the situation is even murkier. The *Goldstone Report* suggests that Israel cannot lawfully fight Hamas rockets by wholesale air attacks. Richard Goldstone, in his interviews, has suggested that Israel should protect itself from these unlawful attacks by more proportionate retail measures, such as commando raids and targeted killing of terrorists engaged in the firing of rockets. Well, there could be no better example of a proportionate, retail, and focused attack on a combatant who was deeply involved in the rocket attacks on Israel, than the killing of Mahmoud al-Mabhouh. Not only was Mabhouh the commander in charge of Hamas's unlawful military actions at the time of his death, he was also personally responsible for the kidnapping and cold-blooded murder of two Israeli soldiers several years earlier.

Obviously it would have been better if he could have been captured and subjected to judicial justice. But it was impossible to capture him, especially when he was in Dubai. If Israel was responsible for the killing, it had only two options: to let him go on his way and continue to endanger Israeli civilian lives by transferring unlawful antipersonnel weapons from Iran to Gaza, or to kill him. There was no third alternative. Given those two options, killing seems like the least tragic choice available.

I leave to others, more expert in these matters, whether if Israel ordered the killing, it was strategically the right thing, or whether they carried it off in an intelligent manner. But as to the legal and moral right to end the threat posed by this mass murderer, the least bad alternative would seem to be his extrajudicial killing.

9

Israel's Actions in Intercepting the Turkish Flotilla Were Entirely Lawful though Perhaps Unwise

June 1, 2010

D URING THE EVENING of May 30, 2010, the Israeli navy intercepted the six ships of the self-anointed "Gaza Freedom Flotilla" organized by two allegedly charitable organizations, the Free Gaza Movement and the Turkish Foundation for Human Rights and Freedoms and Humanitarian Relief (IHH).[1] The Israeli navy shadowed the fleet for several hours, repeatedly entreating the ships' captains to sail for the port of Ashdod where their cargo could be inspected and then delivered by land to Gaza.

These offers were ignored, and during the early morning of May 31, Israeli naval commandos boarded the ships to commandeer them and steer them away from the Gazan coastline. Israeli forces were armed with paintball guns, stun grenades, and side arms which they were instructed to use only in the case of emergency. The passengers aboard five

---

1 IHH in particular has long-standing ties to Hamas and is part of the Union for Good, which explicitly supports suicide bombings.

of the six ships offered no resistance and were apprehended peacefully by Israeli soldiers. However, a group of hardcore IHH members on board the Turkish ship MV *Mavi Marmara* attacked Israeli commandos. Nine activists were subsequently killed by Israeli forces as they attempted to gain control of the ship.

Although the wisdom of Israel's actions in stopping the Gaza flotilla is open to question, the legality of its actions is not. What Israel did was entirely consistent with both international and domestic law. In order to understand why Israel acted within its rights, the complex events at sea must be deconstructed.

First, there is the Israeli blockade of Gaza, which included a naval blockade. Recall that when Israel ended its occupation of Gaza, it did not impose a blockade. Indeed it left behind agricultural facilities in the hope that the newly liberated Gaza Strip would become a peaceful and productive area. Instead Hamas seized control over Gaza and engaged in acts of warfare against Israel. These acts of warfare featured antipersonnel rockets, nearly ten thousand of them, directed at Israeli civilians. This was not only an act of warfare, it was a war crime. Israel responded to the rockets by declaring a blockade, the purpose of which was to assure that no rockets, or other material that could be used for making war against Israeli civilians, was permitted into Gaza. Israel allowed humanitarian aid through its checkpoints. Egypt as well participated in the blockade. There was never a humanitarian crisis in Gaza, merely a shortage of certain goods that would end if the rocket attacks ended.

The legality of blockades as a response to acts of war is not subject to serious doubt. When the United States blockaded Cuba during the missile crisis, the State Department issued an opinion declaring the blockade to be lawful. This, despite the fact that Cuba had not engaged in any act of belligerency against the United States. Other nations have similarly enforced naval blockades to assure their own security.

The second issue is whether it is lawful to enforce a legal blockade in international waters. Again, law and practice are clear. If there is no doubt that the offending ships have made a firm determination to break the blockade, then the blockade may be enforced *before* the offending ships cross the line into domestic waters. Again the United States and other Western countries have frequently boarded ships at high sea in order to assure their security.

Third, were those on board the flotilla innocent non-combatants or did they lose that status once they agreed to engage in the military act of breaking the blockade? Let there be no mistake about the purpose of this flotilla. It was decidedly *not* to provide humanitarian aid to the residents of Gaza, but rather to break the entirely lawful Israeli military blockade. The proof lies in the fact that both Israel and Egypt offered to have all the food, medicine, and other humanitarian goods sent to Gaza, if the boats agreed to land in an Israeli or Egyptian port. That humanitarian offer was soundly rejected by the leaders of the flotilla who publicly announced:

> This mission is not about delivering humanitarian supplies, it's about breaking Israel's siege on 1.5 million Palestinians.[2]

The act of breaking a military siege is itself a military act, and those knowingly participating in such military action put in doubt their status as noncombatants.

2 "Gaza Aid Fleet Undeterred as Israel Steps Up Warnings," *AFP*, 27 May 2010.

It is a close question whether civilians who agree to participate in the breaking of a military blockade have become combatants. They are certainly something different than pure, innocent civilians, and perhaps they are also somewhat different from pure armed combatants. They fit uncomfortably onto the continuum of civilianality that has come to characterize asymmetrical warfare.

Finally, we come to the issue of the right of self-defense engaged in by Israeli soldiers who were attacked by activists on the boat. There can be little doubt that the moment any person on the boat picked up a weapon and began to attack Israeli soldiers boarding the vessel, they lost their status as innocent civilians. Even if that were not the case, under ordinary civilian rules of self-defense, every Israeli soldier had the right to protect himself and his colleagues from attack by knife- and pipe-wielding assailants. Lest there be any doubt that Israeli soldiers were under attack, simply view the accompanying video and watch as so-called peaceful activists repeatedly pummel Israeli soldiers with metal rods (see https://www.youtube.com/watch?v=gYjkLUcbJwo). Every individual has the right to repel such attacks by the use of lethal force, especially when the soldiers were so outnumbered on the deck of the ship. Recall that Israel's rules of engagement required its soldiers to fire only paintballs unless their lives were in danger. Would any country in the world deny its soldiers the right of self-defense under comparable circumstances?

Notwithstanding the legality of Israel's actions, the international community has once again ganged up on Israel. In doing so, Israel's critics have failed to pinpoint precisely what Israel did that allegedly violates international law. Some have wrongly focused on the blockade itself. Others have erroneously pointed to the location of the boarding in international waters. Most have simply pointed to the deaths of so-called peace activists, though these deaths appear to be the result of lawful acts of self-defense. None of these factors alone warrant condemnation, but the end result surely deserves scrutiny by Israeli policy makers. There can be little doubt that the mission was a failure, as judged by its results. It is important, however, to distinguish between faulty policies on the one hand, and alleged violations of international law on the other hand. Only the latter would warrant international intervention, and the case has simply not been made that Israel violated international law.

IO

Why Israel Must Remain Strong

June 4, 2013

FAREED ZAKARIA recently explained why neither side in the Syrian conflict is likely to surrender: "People fight to the end because they know that losers in such wars get killed or 'ethnically cleansed.'"

In this kind of war the words "ethnically cleansed" do not mean displaced or made refugees. They mean, as Zakaria further explained, massacred: "Then you have phase 2, which is the massacre of the Alawites, the 14 percent of Syria that has ruled and that will be a bloodbath."

Nor will the massacres and bloodbaths be limited to combatants, or even civilian officials, if the past is any indication. Babies, women, the elderly, and everyone else will become targets of the vengeful bloodlust.

Already somewhere between eighty thousand and one hundred thousand Syrians have been killed, the vast majority of them civilians.[1] According to United Nations investigators, some have been killed by chemical weapons and thermobaric bombs (which suck the oxygen out of the lungs of everyone in the area.)

[1] The figure is now closer to 200,000; see Laura Smith-Spark, "With More Than 191,000 Dead in Syria, U.N. Rights Chief Slams Global 'Paralysis'," *CNN*, 22 August 2014.

There have been at least seventeen massacres between mid-January and mid-May of this year alone, and there is no sign that the bloodshed is abating. Whether the death toll is closer to eighty thousand or one hundred thousand, this figure is more than all the people killed in nearly a century of conflict between Israel and its enemies—a conflict that includes half a dozen wars and thousands of acts of terrorism and reprisals.

Even if one credits the worst allegations against the nation-state of the Jewish people, Israel has killed fewer civilians since it came into existence sixty-five years ago than any country in history facing comparable threats over so long a time frame.

The world seems unaware of this remarkable fact because the media and international organizations focus far more on Arab and Muslim deaths caused by Israel than on those caused by fellow Arabs and Muslims.

Neither is Syria the first bloody battleground on which Arabs have massacred Arabs and Muslims have massacred Muslims. Black September in Jordan, the protracted war between Iran and Iraq, the civil war in Lebanon, and the killings in post-Saddam Iraq are only some of the bloodiest battles that resulted in many thousands of civilian deaths.

Imagine then what would happen if Israel were ever to lose a war with its Arab and Muslim enemies (as it almost did when it was attacked on Yom Kippur in 1973 by the Egyptian and Syrian armies).

The hatred directed against Jews in general and Israel in particular by Israel's enemies is far more malignant than the animosity between Sunni and Shia Muslims or between Muslim and Christian Arabs. It is taught in schools, preached in mosques, and repeated in the media. There would be no mercy shown. Israeli armies would not be allowed to surrender and be repatriated, as the Egyptian army was when it was trapped in Sinai at the end of the 1973 war.

Israeli civilians would be targeted as they already have been by Hamas and Hezbollah rockets fired in the direction of large population centers. The goal of the war against Israel was expressed by one of its leaders, who proclaimed: "we will exterminate you, until the last one."[2] The desire for revenge has only grown over the course of further warfare and more defeats.

All Israelis live under the grim shadow of this reality. Nor do they count on timely outside intervention to prevent massacres. Remember, this is a nation built on the memory of the Holocaust, during which the world—including the United States, Great Britain, and Canada—shut their gates on those seeking to escape genocide.

That is why Israel will never surrender and will always fight to the end. That is why Israel needs a nuclear deterrent, unsatisfactory as it may be in a part of the world where suicide in the name of Islam is a virtue to so many of Israel's enemies. That is why Israel must always maintain a preventive option, whereby it attacks the enemy military that is poised to attack Israeli civilians. That is why Israel must always maintain qualitative military superiority over the combined resources of its enemies.

This is also why Israel should make every reasonable effort to make peace with the Palestinians, as it has with the Egyptians and the Jordanians, but without sacrificing its security and its ability to successfully resist attack.

The first duty of every democracy is to protect its civilians against enemy attack. Thus far, Israel, though vastly outnumbered, has done a good job. The changes now occurring

2 See https://www.youtube.com/watch?v=UJNdDzweqbY.

in the Arab and Muslim world make Israel's future some-what less certain, as does Iran's movement toward nuclear weaponry capable of inflicting a second Holocaust on Israel's six million Jews and one million Arabs.

Yet so many in the international community seem un-sympathetic to Israel's situation. Whenever it seeks to defend its civilians by attacking military targets, though inadver-tently killing some civilians on occasion, there is a dispro-portional outcry against the Jewish state. Selective boycotts, divestment, and other sanctions are directed only at Israel by people ranging from Alice Walker to Steven Hawking.

Israel must not allow these immorally selective threats of delegitimation to deter it from protecting its citizens against the threat of Syrian-type massacres.

11

Hamas—Not Israel—Killed BBC Reporter's Baby

March 13, 2013

T HE RECENT DISCLOSURE that Omar Misharawi, the baby son of BBC reporter Jihad Misharawi, was actually killed by an errant Hamas rocket rather than by an Israeli missile, should have absolutely no moral implications.

Of course the baby was killed by Hamas.

He would have been killed by Hamas even if the missile that ended his life had been fired by Israel. Hamas is totally and wholly responsible for this death, as it is responsible for every civilian death in Gaza and in Israel. It is Hamas that always begins the battle by firing rockets at Israeli civilians.

Generally Israel does not respond.

When it does, its rockets occasionally kill Palestinian civilians. That's because Hamas wants Palestinians civilians—especially babies—to be killed by Israeli rockets. They want Palestinian babies to be killed precisely so that they can display the kind of photographs that were shown around the world: a grieving father holding his dead baby, presumably killed by an Israeli rocket.

For years, I have called this Hamas's "dead baby strategy." The recent United Nations finding simply confirms the reality of this cynical strategy.

The errant rocket that killed Omar Misharawi was fired by Hamas terrorists from a densely populated civilian area adjacent to the home of the BBC reporter Jihad Misharawi. Hamas selects such locations for firing its rockets precisely so that Israel will respond by firing into civilian areas and killing Palestinian civilians.

They regard such dead civilians as "shahids," or martyrs for the cause. It is better for Hamas's publicity campaign if the rocket that kills the Palestinian baby was fired by the Israeli Defense Forces, but even if the rocket was fired by Hamas terrorists, Hamas will claim, as they do regarding this death, that the lethal rocket was fired by Israel.

Often the evidence is inconclusive, though the forensic evidence in this case points clearly to a Hamas rocket.

The important point is that it doesn't really matter who actually fired the rocket that killed the baby. The baby was killed by Hamas as part of a calculated strategy designed to point the emotional finger of moral blame at the IDF for doing what every democracy would do: namely, defend its civilians from rocket attacks by targeting those who are firing the rockets, even if they are firing them from civilian areas.

Babies like Omar Misharawi will continue to die in Gaza and in Israel so long as the world media continues to serve as facilitators of Hamas's dead baby strategy. Every time a picture of a dead Palestinian baby being held by his grieving parents appears on television or on the front pages of newspapers around the world, Hamas wins. And when Hamas wins, they continue with their deadly strategy.

The media, therefore, is complicit in the death of Omar

Misharawi as it is in the deaths of other civilians who are victims of Hamas's dead baby strategy. Pictures of dead babies in the arms of their grieving fathers are irresistible to the media. That won't change. What should change is the caption.

Every time a dead Palestinian baby is shown, the caption should explain the strategy that led to his or her death: namely that Hamas deliberately fires its rockets from areas in which babies live and into which Israel must fire if it is to stop its own babies from being killed.

It may sound heartless to claim that Hamas wants its own babies to be killed as part of its strategy of demonizing Israel. But there is no escaping the reality and truth of this phenomenon. Indeed it has been admitted by Hamas leaders such as Fathi Hammad:

> For the Palestinian people, death has become an industry, at which women excel, and so do all the people living on this land. The elderly excel at this, and so do the mujahideen and the children. This is why they have formed human shields of the women, the children, the elderly, and the mujahideen, in order to challenge the Zionist bombing machine. It is as if they were saying to the Zionist enemy: 'We desire death like you desire life.'

Of course these Hamas leaders don't desire their own death. They build shelters for themselves and for the terrorists who fire the rockets at Israeli civilians. As soon as these rockets are fired from crowded civilian areas, the terrorists scurry into belowground shelters, leaving babies, women, and other civilians in the path of Israeli rockets that target the rocket launchers.

This isn't martyrdom by the leaders and terrorists. It is cowardice. That too is part of the dead baby strategy: make martyrs of babies while the leaders and terrorists hide in shelters.

In Israel, it is precisely the opposite: shelters are for civilians; soldiers put themselves in harm's way.

12

UN-Palestine Vote Poses Major Threats for Israel

December 1, 2012

T HE GENERAL ASSEMBLY VOTE declaring that Palestine, within the pre-1967 borders, is a state, at least for some purposes, would have nasty legal implications if it were ever to be taken seriously by the international community.

It would mean that Israel, which captured some Jordanian territory after Jordan attacked West Jerusalem in 1967, is illegally occupying the Western Wall (Judaism's holiest site), the Jewish Quarter of old Jerusalem (where Jews have lived for thousands of years), the access road to the Hebrew University (which was established well before Israel even became a state), and other areas necessary to the security of its citizens.

It would also mean that Security Council Resolution 242, whose purpose it was to allow Israel to hold on to some of the territories captured during its defensive 1967 war, would be overruled by a General Assembly vote—something the United Nations Charter explicitly forbids. It would be the first time in history that a nation was required to return all land lawfully captured in a defensive war.

If all the territory captured by Israel in its defensive war is being illegally occupied, then it might be open to the newly recognized Palestinian state to try to bring a case before the International Criminal Court against Israeli political and military leaders who are involved in the occupation. This would mean that virtually every Israeli leader could be placed on trial. What this would entail realistically is that they could not travel to countries that might extradite them for trial in The Hague.

These absurd conclusions follow from the theater of the absurd that occurred when the General Assembly, for the thousandth time, issued an irrelevantly one-sided declaration on Palestine. As Abba Eban once put it: "If Algeria introduced a General Assembly resolution that the world was flat and that Israel had flattened it, it would pass 100 to 10 with 50 abstentions." That's pretty much what happened the other day. I wonder whether the European countries that voted for the resolution knew what a tangled web they were weaving.

Nor was this resolution a recognition of the two-state solution, since a considerable number of states who voted for it have refused to recognize Israel's right to exist. What they were looking for was a one-state resolution—that one state being yet another Islamic country that voted for Hamas in the last election and that is likely to be governed by Sharia law that will not allow Jews or Christians equal rights.

Neither will the General Assembly's actions move the Palestinians closer to accepting the ongoing Israeli offer to begin negotiations toward a two-state solution with no prior conditions. The Palestinians now have little incentive to negotiate a state, which would require considerable compromise and sacrifice on all sides. They now think they can get their state recognized without the need to give up the right of return or to make the kinds of territorial compromises necessary for Israel's security. The United Nations action will only discourage the Palestinians from entering into serious negotiations with Israel.

The United Nations' action will also incentivize Hamas to continue firing rockets into Israel on a periodic basis in order to provoke Israeli retaliation. Many in Hamas believe that the recent fighting in Gaza actually helped the Palestinians get more votes in the General Assembly. They are certainly taking some of the credit for these votes.

All in all, the United Nations vote will make it harder to achieve a peaceful two-state solution acceptable to both sides. But that has been the history of General Assembly actions with regard to Israel, beginning with the lopsided vote in 1975 that challenged Israel's very existence by declaring Zionism—the national liberation movement of the Jewish people—to be a form of racism.

Although the General Assembly was ultimately pressured into rescinding that blood libel, its bigoted spirit still hovers over numerous United Nations agencies that continue to regard Israel as a pariah. It could be felt in the General Assembly hall when so many countries that refused to recognize Israel voted to recognize Palestine.

This is all a prescription for continued warfare, lawfare, and enmity. It is not a prescription for resolving a complex and difficult issue in a realistic manner. But what else is new at the United Nations!

13

A Settlement Freeze Can
Advance Israeli-Palestinian Peace

June 3, 2012

Israel's new unity government is strong and diverse enough to survive a walkout by extremist elements.
Now that Israel has a broad and secure national unity
government, the time is ripe for that government to make a
bold peace offer to the Palestinian Authority.

The Palestinian Authority refuses to negotiate unless
Israel accepts a freeze on settlement building in the West
Bank. Israel accepted a ten-month freeze in 2009, but the
Palestinian Authority didn't come to the bargaining table until weeks before the freeze expired. Its negotiators demanded
that the freeze be extended indefinitely. When Israel refused,
they walked away from the table.

There is every reason to believe that they would continue
such game-playing if the Israeli government imposed a similar freeze now, especially in light of current efforts by the
Palestinian Authority and Hamas to form their own unity
government, which would likely include elements opposed
to any negotiation with the Jewish state.

That is why Prime Minister Benjamin Netanyahu
should now offer a conditional freeze: Israel will stop

all settlement building in the West Bank as soon as the Palestinian Authority sits down at the bargaining table, and the freeze will continue as long as the talks continue in good faith.

The first issue on the table should be the rough borders of a Palestinian state. Setting those would require recognizing that the West Bank can be realistically divided into three effective areas:

- Those that are relatively certain to remain part of Israel, such as Ma'ale Adumim, Gilo, and other areas close to the center of Jerusalem.

- Those that are relatively certain to become part of a Palestinian state, such as Ramallah, Jericho, Jenin, and the vast majority of the heavily populated Arab areas of the West Bank beyond Israel's security barrier.

- Those reasonably in dispute, including some of the large settlement blocs several miles from Jerusalem such as Ariel (which may well remain part of Israel, but subject to negotiated land swaps).

This rough division is based on prior negotiations and on positions already articulated by each side. If there can be agreement concerning this preliminary division—even tentative or conditional—then the settlement-building dispute would quickly disappear.

There would be no Israeli building in those areas likely to become part of a Palestinian state. There would be no limit on Israeli building within areas likely to remain part of Israel. And the conditional freeze would continue in disputed areas until it was decided which would remain part of Israel and which would become part of the new

Palestinian state. As portions of the disputed areas are allocated to Palestine or Israel, the building rules would reflect that ongoing allocation.

I recently proposed this idea to a high-ranking Israeli official. His initial reaction was mostly positive, but he insisted that it would be difficult to impose an absolute building freeze in any areas in which Israelis currently live. He pointed out that families grow and that new bedrooms and bathrooms are needed in existing structures as a simple matter of humanitarian needs. I reminded him that Mr. Netanyahu has repeatedly stated that Israel is prepared to make "painful compromises" in the interests of peace.

An absolute building freeze would be such a painful but necessary compromise. It might also encourage residents of settlements deep in the West Bank to move to areas that will remain part of Israel, especially if the freeze were accompanied by financial inducements to relocate.

Such a proposal by Israel would be an important first step and a good test of the bona fides of the Palestinian side. Since their precondition to negotiation will have been met by the promise of a freeze (to begin the moment they sit down to negotiate), they would have no further excuse for refusing the Israeli offer to try to resolve the conflict.

The conditional freeze would also test the bona fides of the Israeli government, which would no longer have the excuse that any freeze would risk toppling a fragile coalition that relies on right-wingers who have threatened to withdraw in the event of another freeze. The new national unity government is now sufficiently large and diverse that it could now survive a walkout by elements opposed to any freeze.

Once the parties reach a preliminary agreement regarding the three areas and what could be built where, they could get down to the nitty-gritty of working on compromises to produce an enduring peace.

These compromises will require the Israelis to give up claims to areas of the West Bank that were part of biblical Israel but that are heavily populated by Palestinians. It will require the Palestinians to give up any claim to a massive "right of return" for the millions of descendants of those who once lived in what is now Israel. It will require an agreement over Jerusalem, plus assurances about Israel's security in the Jordan Valley and in areas that could pose the threat of rocket attacks like those that have come from the Gaza Strip in recent years.

Both sides say they want peace. In my conversations with both Israeli and Palestinian leaders, I have repeatedly heard the view that "everyone" knows what a pragmatic compromise resolution will look like. Each side claims that the other side has erected artificial barriers to reaching that resolution.

If the building freeze issue can be taken off the table, one of the most controversial and divisive barriers will have been eliminated. The Israeli government should take the first step, but the Palestinian Authority must take the second step by immediately sitting down to negotiate in good faith.

14

Mideast Peace Talks
Should Resume

November 2, 2012

I WAS INVITED to meet with President Mahmoud
Abbas of the Palestinian Authority just before he spoke
to the General Assembly of the United Nations. I
came to the meeting with an agenda: to persuade him to sit
down with the Israelis and resume negotiations without first
requiring the Israelis to accept a total settlement freeze.

I knew the Israelis would not—indeed could not—agree
to a settlement freeze as a prior condition to beginning negotiations, since they had previously agreed to a nine-month
freeze and the Palestinians refused to come to the bargaining
table until just before the freeze expired, and then demanded
that the freeze be extended.

Prime Minister Benjamin Netanyahu had invited the
Palestinians to begin negotiations with no prior conditions—
an invitation that the Palestinians had rejected because the
Israelis refused first to impose a freeze.

My proposal to President Abbas was to have the
Palestinian Authority agree to sit down and begin negotiations before any freeze began, if the Israelis would agree
to begin a freeze only after the negotiations commenced

in good faith. In that way, the Israelis would get what they wanted: negotiations beginning with no prior actions on their part. And the Palestinians would get what they wanted: a settlement freeze while the negotiations continued in good faith.

I had written an op-ed laying out my plan, and I brought a copy of it to my meeting with Abbas. When I showed it to him, he said, "This looks good," and he passed it on to Saeb Erekat, his close adviser. Erekat read it closely and gave it back to Abbas, who circled the operative paragraph and signed it, "Abu Mazzen." He asked me to show it to Netanyahu, with whom I would be meeting several days later.

Between the time I met with President Abbas and the time I met with Prime Minister Netanyahu, both delivered their speeches to the General Assembly. Netanyahu reiterated his invitation to sit down and negotiate a peaceful resolution, while Abbas made a belligerent speech accusing Israel of ethnic cleansing and other crimes.

He expressed no real interest in negotiating peace. So when I told Netanyahu about Abbas's apparent acceptance of my proposal, he was understandably skeptical. But he took a copy of the signed article and put it in his pocket, saying he would certainly give it careful consideration.

Since that time, Abbas has indicated that he might be willing to sit down and negotiate without a settlement freeze, but only after the United Nations votes on upgrading the status of the Palestinian Authority. Netanyahu, during his recent visit to France, reiterated a desire to sit down and negotiate with no preconditions.

There are no real downsides for either the Palestinians or the Israelis in resuming negotiations. Everyone knows roughly what a negotiated peace would look like.

There would be some mutually agreed upon territorial changes to the 1967 borders, a demilitarized Palestinian state, some military presence along the Jordan River to assure Israel's security, a realistic resolution of the Jerusalem issue, and an abandonment of the so-called right of return. There would be no immediate resolution of the Gaza issue, so long as Hamas remained opposed to Israel's right to exist.

Peace between Israel and the Palestinian Authority is long overdue. The parties have come close on several occasions. Hopefully, the time will soon be right for moving in the direction of peace. I hope my proposal will help to facilitate renewed negotiations.

15

Terrorists Win with Israel Prisoner Swap

October 13, 2011

T HE DECISION by the Israeli government to release hundreds of properly convicted Palestinian terrorists in exchange for one illegally kidnapped Israeli soldier, understandable as it is emotionally, dramatically illustrates why terrorism works.

By agreeing to this exchange, Israel has once again shown its commitment to saving the life of even one kidnapped soldier, regardless of the cost. And the cost here is extremely high, because some of the released terrorists will almost certainly try to kill again.

Leaders of terrorist groups, such as Hamas and Hezbollah, fully understand this cruel arithmetic of death. As Hassan Nasrallah, the head of Hezbollah, put it: "We are going to win because they love life and we love death."

Democratic societies that value the life of each citizen are more vulnerable to emotional blackmail than terrorist groups that are steeped in the culture of death.

Terrorists understand what history has shown: that democratic societies, regardless of what they say about not negotiating with terrorists, will, in the end, submit to emotional blackmail: they will release their terrorist prisoners in order to obtain the release of their own kidnapped or hijacked citizens.

Accordingly, the threat of deterrence against terrorists is weak, because every terrorist knows that regardless of the prison sentence he receives, there is a high likelihood that he will be released well before he has served it. This not only encourages more terrorism, but it also incentivizes kidnappings and hijackings that provide the terrorist with hostages to exchange for captured terrorists.

Accordingly, from a pure cost-benefit perspective, it may well be wrong to agree to such disproportionate exchanges. But democracies do not operate solely on a cost-benefit basis because the families of kidnapped or hijacked citizens have a right to present their emotional case in the court of public opinion, as Gilad Shalit's family, especially his mother, so effectively did. They can influence policy against a simple cost-benefit calculation and in favor of a more humanistic approach.

Contrast the pleas of the Shalit family with the plea of Zahra Maladan. Maladan is an educated woman who edits a women's magazine in Lebanon. She is also a mother who undoubtedly loves her son. She has ambitions for him, but they are different from those of most mothers in the West. She wants her son to become a suicide bomber.

At the funeral for the assassinated Hezbollah terrorist Imad Mugniyah—the mass murderer responsible for killing 241 marines in 1983 and more than 100 women, children, and men in Buenos Aires in 1992 and 1994—Ms. Maladan was quoted in the *New York Times* offering the following admonition to her son: "If you're not going to follow the steps of the Islamic resistance martyrs, then I don't want you."

Nor is Ms. Maladan alone in urging her children to become suicide murderers. Umm Nidal, who ran for the

Palestinian Legislative Council, prepared all of her sons for martyrdom. She has ten sons, one of whom already engaged in a suicide operation, which she considered "a blessing, not a tragedy." She is now preparing to "sacrifice them all."

It is impossible, of course, to generalize about cultures. There was genuine joy among many in Gaza when the deal was announced and when it became evident that their loved ones, despite their terrorist activities, would be returned.

All decent people love their children and want them to live good lives. It is their leaders who prefer death over life and who make them feel guilty for not acting on that perverse preference. Democratic leaders, on the other hand, urge their citizens to act in the interests of life and see death as a necessary evil in fighting against even greater evils.

While the preference for life over death may appear to be a weakness in the ability of democracies to fight against terrorism, in the end it is a strength. It is a strength because it signals a democracy's commitment to value the life of every single one of its citizens.

Israeli and American soldiers go into battle knowing that their countries will do everything in their power to rescue them, even if it means taking extraordinary risks. Nations that are committed to such humanistic values tend to have superior armies, as the United States and Israel do.

An important goal of terrorists is to force democracies to surrender their humanistic values. Israel, by agreeing to exchange hundreds of terrorists for one soldier, has shown the world that it will not compromise on its value system, which proclaims that he who saves one human being, it is as if he has saved the world.

16

Israel's Right to Self-Defense Against Hamas

November 18, 2012

AS HAMAS CONTINUES to target Israeli civilians in their homes, Israel continues to target terrorist leaders and other legitimate military targets. Hamas has now succeeded in killing a family of three[1] in their home. Targeting civilians, such as that family, is a calculated Hamas policy designed to sow terror among the Israeli population. Hamas supporters celebrate the murder of Jewish civilians. Every rocket fired by Hamas from one of its own civilian areas at a nonmilitary Israeli target is a double war crime that should be universally condemned by all reasonable people. Israel's response—targeting only terrorists and Hamas military leaders—is completely lawful and legitimate. It constitutes an act of self-defense pursuant to Article 51 of the United Nations Charter and universally accepted principles of international law.

There is absolutely no comparison between the murderous war crimes being committed by Hamas and the lawful targeting of terrorists by the Israeli military. Yet the Egyptian

---

1 "Live Blog: Day 2 of Israel-Gaza Conflict 2012," *Haaretz*, 15 November 2012.

government, now controlled by the Muslim Brotherhood, has condemned Israel while remaining relatively silent about Hamas. This should not be surprising, since Hamas is an offshoot of the Muslim Brotherhood. (The Muslim Brotherhood no longer controls Egypt.)

Some in the media also insist on describing the recent events in Gaza as "a cycle of violence" without distinguishing between the war crimes committed by Hamas and the lawful actions undertaken by Israel to protect its citizens against such war crimes. It would be as if the media described lawful police efforts to stop illegal drug-related murders as a "cycle of violence." Yet J Street, an organization that persists in calling itself pro-Israel, insists on describing the situation in Gaza as a "spiral of violence."[2]

What would Egypt do if Hamas or Islamic Jihad suddenly began to lob deadly shells in the direction of Cairo suburbs? What would any country do? President Obama was entirely correct in defending Israel's right[3] to protect its citizens from terrorist attacks and in condemning Hamas for initiating these attacks. He is also correct in calling for Israel to try its best to avoid unnecessary civilian casualties, as Israel has always done and continues to do. The targeted killing of Hamas military commander Ahmed al-Jabari is a case in point. He and a Hamas associate were killed in a pinpoint airstrike that apparently caused no collateral damage.

There are some who argue, quite absurdly, that all targeted assassination is unlawful, since it constitutes extrajudicial killing. But all military deaths are extrajudicial killings, as are deaths caused in the civilian context by

2 "Reaction to Escalation of Violence in Israel and Gaza," *J Street*, 15 November 2012.

3 Barak Ravid, "Obama Works to Avert Israel-Egypt Break as Gaza Violence Persists," *Haaretz*, 15 November 2012.

individual acts of self-defense or by the police shooting a dangerous fleeing felon. In fact, only Israel among all the countries of the world has subjected its policy of targeted killing of terrorists to judicial review. The Israeli Supreme Court has set out careful and precise criteria for when targeted killing is appropriate and which people constitute appropriate targets under international law. Ahmed Jabari plainly fits within those criteria.

Israel's response to the Hamas rockets must of course be proportional, but proportionality does not require that Israel wait until a large number of its civilians are actually killed or seriously injured. Israel's response must be proportionate to the threat faced by its civilian population. Indeed, the goal of its actions must be to prevent even a single Israeli civilian death.

In addition to the Israel Supreme Court imposing constraints on its military, Israeli civilians and the Israeli media also serve as an important check. When, on occasion, Israeli military actions have caused a disproportionate number of civilian deaths, Israelis have become outraged at their military and demanded a greater adherence to the principles of proportionality. This contrasts sharply with the population of Gaza, much of which applauds and celebrates every time an Israeli child is killed by a Hamas rocket. It is immoral in the extreme to compare Israel to Gaza or to compare the Israeli military to Hamas terrorists.

It would be better, of course, if a permanent cease-fire could be arranged under which Hamas would stop firing rockets at civilians and Israel would no longer need to target Hamas terrorists. Egypt could play a more positive role by trying to bring about a cease-fire instead of unilaterally condemning the victims of war crimes, as it has done.

But until Hamas stops terrorizing more than a million Israeli civilians, the Israeli military will have no choice other than to use its technological advantage to prevent and deter Hamas terrorism. It is the obligation of every sovereign state, first and foremost, to protect its civilian population from terrorist attacks. Israel's decision to use targeted assassination against Hamas combatants is preferable to other military options, such as a massive ground attack that inevitably will cause more collateral damage.

But if Hamas's rocket attacks persist, Israel may have little choice but to invade Gaza and take more extensive steps to protect its civilian population. It is up to Hamas, which is entirely to blame for the current situation, as it was when Israel was forced to invade back in 2008. The international community and the media must begin to differentiate between war crimes committed by terrorists and legitimate acts of self-defense engaged in by a responsible national military. Failing to emphasize that distinction encourages terrorism and erodes the moral basis of the important principle of just warfare.

17

The Palestinian Leadership Is Responsible for the Continuing Israeli Occupation of the West Bank

December 10, 2010

THE DECISION by the Obama administration to stop pressuring Israel to end the West Bank settlements in order to get the Palestinian leadership to return to the negotiations table should not obscure the following sad reality: the fact that the Israeli occupation of the West Bank has not ended is largely, if not entirely, the fault of the Palestinian leadership. This may sound counterintuitive, since it is Israel that is continuing to occupy the West Bank, but it has been the Palestinian leadership that has repeatedly refused to accept Israel's offers to end the occupation. It was recently revealed that in 2008, the Israeli government again offered to end the occupation, and once again the Palestinian leadership failed to accept the offer. This is what the Associated Press reported on November 27, 2010:

> Since leaving office, [Former Israeli Prime Minister Ehud] Olmert has confirmed that he made Israel's

most far-reaching offer to the Palestinians, proposing a Palestinian state on close to 94 percent of the West Bank and offering the equivalent of the final 6 percent of territory in a land "swap."

Olmert said yesterday that the Palestinians never responded to his offer, made in the final months of his term in office.

"I think that they made a mistake."

Yasser Arafat made the same mistake in 2000 and 2001 when he refused a similar offer from Israeli prime minister Ehud Barak and United States president Bill Clinton.

In 2005 when Israeli prime minister Ariel Sharon completely ended the occupation of the Gaza Strip, Hamas responded by showering thousands of rockets on Israeli civilian targets.

And now in 2010 the Palestinian leadership is refusing to sit down and negotiate with the Netanyahu government unless Israel accepts preconditions.

This reminds me of what Abba Eban famously said after Israel won a decisive war started by the Arabs in 1967:

"This was the first war in history that on the morrow the victors sued for peace and the vanquished called for unconditional surrender."

It is no wonder that so many Israeli citizens are skeptical about whether the Palestinian leadership is willing to make, or capable of actually making peace with Israel. This skepticism has been fueled by a recent article on the official website of the Palestinian Authority claiming that there is no hard evidence of any Jewish connection to the Western Wall, Judaism's holiest site. Instead, it claims that "this wall is the place where the Prophet Muhammad tethered his winged steed, Buraq, during his miraculous overnight journey from Mecca to Jerusalem in the seventh century." The Palestinian Authority article asserts that "the Al Buraq Wall is the western wall of Al Aksa, which the Zionist occupation falsely claims ownership of and calls the Wailing Wall or Kotel." In other words, the Palestinian leadership expects Israelis to believe Muslim theological claims over Jewish archaeological evidence.

Moreover, the Palestinian Authority refuses to accept Israel as the nation-state of the Jewish people, and refuses to end the repeated incitements against Jews that are a staple of the Palestinian Authority–controlled media.

It is also no wonder that many Israelis have concluded that the Palestinian leadership has marginalized the Palestinians. What can the PA now offer Israel in exchange for the end of the occupation and the division of Jerusalem? Not peace in the north, which is controlled by Iran's wholly owned subsidiary Hezbollah. Not peace in the west, which is controlled by Hamas, another Iranian surrogate. All the Palestinian Authority can now offer Israel is peace on the relatively quiet eastern border. And it would be an uncertain and incomplete peace even with the PA, since there is no assurance that the Palestinian Authority will retain control over the West Bank, and even if it manages to isolate Hamas in Gaza, there is no guarantee that terrorist groups will not use the West Bank as a launching pad for rockets and other forms of terrorism.

The Palestinians have employed two weapons as alternatives to actually sitting down and negotiating a two-state solution. The first was the violence incited by Arafat after he rejected the Barak-Clinton offer of 2000–2001. Instead of continuing to negotiate, Arafat ordered the beginning of a second Intifada with its suicide bombings and the deaths of thousands of Palestinians and Israelis. This tactic got the

Palestinians nothing but bloodshed and the continuing support of the hard left. It lost them the support of the Israeli peace movement and drove many Israeli moderates to the right.

Following Arafat's untimely death—untimely in the sense that if he had died a few years *earlier* the Occupation would have ended by now—the Palestinian Authority shifted from guerilla warfare to guerilla "lawfare."

Under this tactic, the Palestinian Authority has taken advantage of the United Nations' biased machinery of international "human rights" to push Israel into the dock as a criminal state, accusing it of war crimes every time it takes any action in defense of its citizens, whether it be building a security barrier against terrorists, treating terrorists as combatants and targeting them for military attack, or defending its civilians against rocket attacks. This "lawfare" tactic is also backfiring. It is making it more difficult for Israel to end the occupation, because many Israelis fear that leaving the West Bank will bring the same violent response that followed the end of the occupation of Gaza: namely rocket attacks on Israeli civilians. And if Israel were to seek to protect its civilians, as it did in Gaza, it would be accused of war crimes and hauled in front of the International Criminal Court.

A related weapon, now being widely used on university campuses around the world, is to challenge Israel's legitimacy as a state—even within its pre-1967 borders. This tactic too is making it harder for Israel to make peace, because many Israelis fear that any agreement is only a tactic that will lead to further attacks on the legitimacy of the Jewish state and calls for a single binational state, which would inevitably become yet another Muslim Arab state.

To hold the Palestinian leadership responsible for the continuing Israeli occupation of the West Bank is not to blame the victim. The Palestinian people have indeed been victims—of their own leadership and the refusal of so many Palestinians to take yes for an answer when they have been offered an end to the occupation, and have instead chosen violence, lawfare, and rejection of Israel as the nation-state of the Jewish people.

I have long believed and written that when the Palestinian leadership wants their own state *more* than they want the end of the Jewish state, there will be a two-state solution.

The time has come for those Palestinians who seek peace to take control over their own destiny and demand that their leaders sit down, with no preconditions, and negotiate an end to the occupation and the implementation of a two-state solution. If they do not, they too will share the blame for the continuing occupation and lack of statehood.

18

Some Hard Questions
about the Western European
Double Standard Against Israel

March 12, 2014

A S S O M A N Y Western European academics, artists, and
activists try to isolate Israel by imposing boycotts,
divestments, and sanctions (BDS) only against the
nation-state of the Jewish people, the time has come to point
an accusing finger at these accusers and to ask some hard
questions about their underlying biases.

Why are so many of the grandchildren of Nazis and
Nazi collaborators, who brought us the Holocaust, once
again declaring war on the Jews? Why have we seen such an
increase in anti-Semitism and irrationally virulent anti-Zionism in Western Europe? To answer these questions, a myth
must first be exposed. That myth is the one perpetrated
by the French, the Dutch, the Norwegians, the Swiss, the
Belgians, the Austrians, and many other Western Europeans:
namely that the Holocaust was solely the work of German
Nazis aided perhaps by some Polish, Ukrainian, Latvian,
Lithuanian, and Estonian collaborators. False. The Holocaust
was perpetrated by Europeans—by Nazi sympathizers and

collaborators among the French, Dutch, Norwegians, Swiss, Belgians, Austrians, and other Europeans, both western and eastern.

If the French government had not deported to the death camps more Jews than their German occupiers asked for; if so many Dutch and Belgian citizens and government officials had not cooperated in the roundup of Jews; if so many Norwegians had not supported Quisling; if Swiss government officials and bankers had not exploited Jews; if Austria had not been more Nazi than the Nazis; the Holocaust would not have had so many Jewish victims.

In light of the widespread European complicity in the destruction of European Jewry, the pervasive anti-Semitism and irrationally hateful anti-Zionism that has recently surfaced throughout Western Europe should surprise no one.

"Oh no," we hear from European apologists. "This is different. We don't hate the Jews. We only hate their nation-state. Moreover, the Nazis were right-wing. We're left-wing, so we can't be anti-Semites."

Nonsense. The hard left has a history of anti-Semitism as deep and enduring as the hard right. The line from Voltaire, to Karl Marx, to Levrenti Beria, to Robert Faurison, to today's hard-left Israel bashers is as straight as the line from Wilhelm Mars to the persecutors of Alfred Dreyfus to Hitler.

The Jews of Europe have always been crushed between the Black and the Red—victims of extremism whether it be the ultranationalism of Khmelnitsky or the ultra-anti-Semitism of Stalin.

"But some of the most strident anti-Zionists are Jews, such as Norman Finkelstein and even Israelis such as Gilad Atzmon. Surely they can't be anti-Semites."

Why not? Gertrude Stein and Alice Toklas collaborated with the Gestapo.

Atzmon, a hard leftist, describes himself as a proud self-hating Jew and admits that his ideas derive from a notorious anti-Semite. He denies that the Holocaust is historically proven but believes that Jews may well have killed Christian children to use their blood to bake Passover matzo. And he thinks it's "rational" to burn down synagogues.

Finkelstein believes in an international Jewish conspiracy that includes Steven Spielberg, Leon Uris, Eli Wiesel, and Andrew Lloyd Webber! Some of the Soviet Union's leading anti-Semitic propagandists were Jews.

"But Israel is doing bad things to the Palestinians," the European apologists insist, "and we are sensitive to the plight of the underdog."

No you're not! Where are your demonstrations on behalf of the oppressed Tibetans, Georgians, Syrians, Armenians, Kurds, or even Ukrainians? Where are your BDS movements against the Chinese, the Russians, the Cubans, the Turks or the Assad regime? Only the Palestinians, only Israel? Why? Not because the Palestinians are more oppressed than these and other groups. Only because their alleged oppressors are Jews and the nation-state of the Jews. Would there be demonstrations and BDS campaigns on behalf of the Palestinians if they were oppressed by Jordan or Egypt? Oh, wait, the Palestinians were oppressed by Egypt and Jordan. Gaza was an open-air prison between 1948 and 1967 when Egypt was the occupying power. And remember Black September when Jordan killed more Palestinians than Israel did in a century? I don't remember any demonstration or BDS campaigns—because there weren't any. When Arabs occupy or kill Arabs, Europeans go ho hum. But when Israel opens a soda factory in Ma'ale Adumim, which even the Palestinian leadership acknowledges will remain part of Israel in any peace deal, Oxfam (which collaborates with anti-Israel terrorist groups) fires Scarlett Johansson for advertising a company that employs hundreds of Palestinians.

The hypocrisy of so many hard-left Western Europeans would be staggering if it were not so predictable, based on the sordid history of Western Europe's treatment of the Jews.

Even England, which was on the right side of the war against Nazism, has a long history of anti-Semitism, beginning with the expulsion of the Jews in 1290 to the notorious White Paper of 1939 which prevented the Jews of Europe from seeking asylum from the Nazis in British-mandated Palestine.

And Ireland, which vacillated in the war against Hitler, boasts some of the most virulent anti-Israel rhetoric.

The simple reality is that one cannot understand the current Western European left-wing war against the nation-state of the Jewish people without first acknowledging the long-term European war against the Jewish people themselves.

Theodor Herzl understood the pervasiveness and irrationality of European anti-Semitism, which led him to the conclusion that the only solution to Europe's Jewish problem was for European Jews to leave that bastion of Jew hatred and to return to their original homeland, which is now the state of Israel.

None of this is to deny Israel's imperfections or the criticism it justly deserves for some of its policies. But these imperfections and deserved criticism cannot even begin to explain, much less justify, the disproportionate hatred directed against the only nation-state of the Jewish people and the disproportionate silence regarding the far greater imperfections and deserved criticism of other nations and groups—including the Palestinians.

Nor is this to deny that many Western European individuals and some Western European countries have refused to succumb to the hatred against the Jews or their state. The

Czech Republic comes to mind. But far too many Western Europeans are as irrational in their hatred toward Israel as their ancestors were in their hatred toward their Jewish neighbors. As Amos Oz once aptly observed: the walls of his grandparents' Europe were covered with graffiti saying "Jews, go to Palestine." Now they say, "Jews, get out of Palestine"— by which is meant Israel.

Who do these Western European bigots think they're fooling? Only fools who want to be fooled in the interest of denying that they are manifesting new variations on their grandparents' old biases. Any objective person with an open mind, open eyes, and an open heart must see the double standard being applied to the nation-state of the Jewish people by so many of the grandchildren of those who lethally applied a double standard to the Jews of Europe in the 1930s and 1940s. They must be shamed into looking themselves in the mirror of morality and acknowledging their own bigotry.

PART II

OPERATION PROTECTIVE EDGE

Operation Protective Edge

O N JULY 8, 2014, Israel launched Operation Protective Edge to suppress Hamas rocket and mortar fire from the Gaza Strip aimed at Israeli cities, towns, and kibbutzim.

The initial spark behind the escalation in hostilities was the kidnapping of three Israeli teenagers, Naftali Fraenkel, Gilad Shaer, and Eyal Yifrah on June 12 by Hamas-affiliated militants. Israel responded with a series of raids in the West Bank to find the children, which culminated in the arrest of most of Hamas's leadership there. The bodies of the three teenagers were eventually recovered on June 30, but tensions only continued to rise when three Israeli criminals kidnapped and murdered a sixteen-year-old Palestinian boy, Mohammed Abu Khdeir. As Palestinians across the West Bank began rioting, Hamas resumed its rocket attacks on Israel in full force.

In response, on July 8 Prime Minister Netanyahu announced plans to call up forty thousand reservists and authorized the Israeli air force to hit Hamas targets across Gaza. By July 14, following days of Israeli bombardment and nearly two hundred Palestinian deaths, the Egyptian government announced a cease-fire plan backed by Prime Minister Mahmoud Abbas, which was accepted the following day by Israel. Hamas, however, rejected the proposal, demanding the release of its members in the West Bank and a lifting of the blockade on the Gaza Strip.

On July 16, UNRWA, the UN agency charged with supervising the distribution of aid in the Palestinian Territories, issued the first of several reports that Hamas was hiding rockets in its facilities. That night, despite nominally accepting a five-hour humanitarian cease-fire, thirteen armed Hamas operatives were intercepted as they emerged from a tunnel on the Israeli side of the border just one mile from a kibbutz, carrying abduction equipment. The following day, on July 17 Prime Minister Netanyahu ordered ground troops into Gaza arguing that the destruction of tunnels was imperative to maintaining the security of Israeli citizens.

For the next three weeks, Israeli troops maintained a presence in much of the north of the Gaza Strip including several densely populated areas such as Shuja'iyya, Beit Hanoun, and Rafah while they attempted to dismantle the Hamas network of cross-border tunnels. Hamas had deliberately located the entrances in urban areas to complicate Israeli efforts to destroy them. Hamas militants repeatedly fired on Israeli soldiers from civilian buildings, including private homes, hospitals, refugee centers, and mosques. This was the cause of most of the Palestinian civilian casualties over the course of Operation Protective Edge.

Israel implemented numerous short-term humanitarian cease-fires, most notably on July 20, July 25, July 26, and July 30, all of which it respected despite violations by Hamas and other militant groups. On July 31, both Hamas and Israel agreed to a seventy-two-hour cease-fire but only ninety minutes after its implementation on August 1 Hamas gunmen emerged from a tunnel in Rafah, killing two Israeli soldiers and apparently capturing another (that soldier was ultimately declared to have been killed, but Hamas has apparently taken his remains). Israel subsequently announced that it would not negotiate another cease-fire with Hamas until it was satisfied that the tunnels had been destroyed. By August 3, Israeli troops began to pull back, having destroyed more than thirty Hamas tunnels, and on August 5 the IDF announced that there were no Israeli forces left in Gaza. A mutually agreed seventy-two-hour cease-fire took effect that same day.

However, Hamas continued to fire rockets and mortars at Israel, killing a four-year-old Israeli child over the course of the hostilities. They have also executed numerous Palestinian civilians whom they accused of collaborating with Israel. The prospect of a permanent truce remains elusive, as Hamas has repeatedly refused to demilitarize and continues to demand that Israel lift its entire blockade of the Gaza Strip.

It is clear, therefore, that it was Hamas that started the war and that it was Hamas that refused to accept ceasefire proposals that would have ended it much sooner. According to Khalil Shikaki, a respected Palestinian political scientist, Mahmoud Abbas blamed Hamas for having "started the war."[1] Abbas has also blamed Hamas for having prolonged the war by needlessly extending the fighting.[2]

It is clear, therefore, that it was Hamas that started the war and that it was Hamas that refused to accept ceasefire proposals that would have ended it much sooner. According to Khalil Shikaki, a respected Palestinian political scientist, Mahmoud Abbas blamed Hamas for having "started the war."[3] Abbas has also blamed Hamas for having prolonged the war by needlessly extending the fighting.

---

1 Jodi Rudoren, "Palestinian Leader Assails Hamas, Calling Unity Pact into Question," the *New York Times*, 8 September 2014, p. A8.

2 "Palestinian Leader Says Hamas Caused Prolonged War," *USA Today*, 29 August 2014.

3 Jodi Rudoren, "Palestinian Leader Assails Hamas, Calling Unity Pact into Question," the *New York Times*, 8 September 2014, p. A8.

On July 10, 2014, I began to write a series of articles about this conflict and its legal, moral, political, and diplomatic implications. The chapters that appear in this part are based, in part, on those articles.[4]

4 Most of these articles appeared in *Haaretz*, the *Jerusalem Post*, and various online publications.

19

Israel Defends Entire Civilized World

July 10, 2014

ISRAEL'S MILITARY ACTION against Hamas terrorist rockets is a preview of what the entire civilized world is likely to face in the near future.

Islamic militant terrorists—whether they are called ISIS, al-Qaeda, Hamas, or Hezbollah—use or will be using similar tactics. They target civilians while hiding among civilians in order to induce democracies to kill civilians so that the media will show gruesome pictures of dead children and blame these deaths on the democracy, rather than the terrorists who use children and other civilians as human shields.

The democracy is then put to the tragic choice of either allowing terrorist attacks against its own civilians or taking military action that risks the lives of enemy civilians.

That is precisely the choice that Israel has had to make as hundreds of rockets are directed at its cities from densely populated civilian areas in Gaza. Israel has been very careful to try to minimize civilian casualties. They drop leaflets, make phone calls, and even send noisemaking bomblets to warn civilians to leave areas to which rockets are being fired. Mostly the civilians leave. Sometimes they don't. When they don't, the Israeli military does not fire at the rockets, thereby putting their own civilians at risk.

Yet some in the media describe the current situation in Gaza as a "cycle of violence." The reality, of course, is that there is no such cycle. It is a one-way street that Hamas has driven down precisely in order to create the illusion of a cycle with equal blame on both sides.

There is no comparison—legally, morally, diplomatically, or by any other criteria—between what Hamas is doing and how Israel is responding. Hamas is willfully and deliberately committing a double war crime by targeting Israeli civilians and using Palestinian civilians as human shields. The deliberate targeting of civilians, as Hamas admits—indeed boasts— it is doing, is a clear war crime. Hamas has specifically aimed its lethal rockets at Beersheba, Tel Aviv, Haifa, and Jerusalem. This is a war crime.

Moreover, it is firing these rockets from hospitals, schools, and houses in densely populated areas in order to cause Israel to kill Palestinian civilians. This too is a war crime.

I have called this Hamas's "dead baby strategy." It deliberately puts Israel to the tragic choice of attacking the rockets and killing some children who are used as human shields, or refraining from attacking the rockets and thereby placing their own children at risk.

Israel has generally chosen the option of refraining from attacking legitimate military targets, but when any human shields are inadvertently killed or injured, Hamas stands ready to cynically parade the dead civilians in front of television cameras, which transmit these gruesome pictures around the world with captions blaming Israel.

Hamas has also adamantly refused to build bomb shelters for its civilian population. It has built shelters but has limited access to them to Hamas terrorists. This is precisely the opposite of what Israel does—building shelters for its civilians and placing its soldiers in harm's way.

Most recently Hamas has forced or encouraged civilians to stand on the rooftops of military targets so as to prevent Israel from attacking these entirely appropriate targets. Indeed a lawsuit is now being brought in Israel, against the Israeli military, urging it to ignore these human shields and to attack the military targets.

The argument is that unless the military targets are attacked, Israeli civilians will die, and a democracy has the obligation to prefer the lives of its own civilians over the lives of enemy civilians. Thus far the Israeli military has refrained from attacking military targets that are protected by human shields.

Nor was there any symmetry between the kidnapping and brutal murder of three Israeli teenagers by Hamas operatives and the equally despicable killing of an Arab teenager by a handful of Israeli individuals.

The Hamas-inspired kidnapping was part of a long-term Hamas policy. Hamas has built dozens of tunnels between Gaza and Israel for the sole purpose of kidnapping and/or killing Israeli civilians. I have been inside one such tunnel, whose exit was just yards away from an Israeli kindergarten with dozens of children. The killing of the three Israeli teenagers was a result of Hamas's policy, regardless of whether the specific decision to kill the youths was or wasn't made at the top levels of the Hamas leadership.

The killing of the Palestinian youth, to the contrary, was clearly against the wishes of the Israeli government, the Israeli people, and Israeli policy. It was the act of deranged extremists—an act that hurt Israel terribly both internally and externally. Yet many in the international media insist on comparing these two very different atrocities.

The entire civilized world should be standing behind

Israel as it defends itself against war crimes, because what Israel is doing is precisely what every democracy would do if faced with similar threats to its civilian population. That so many continue to support—or remain silent about—those who commit these war crimes tells us something deeply disturbing about their values and prejudices.

The world must come to realize that the major conflict today is between Islamic extremists—such as ISIS, al-Qaeda, and Hamas—who will stop at nothing to achieve their theo-logical-political-military goals, and democracies that must fight these extremists while complying with the rule of law. Israel should be praised for leading the way.

20

The Current Conflict between Israel and Hamas Shatters Myths

July 10, 2014

THE CURRENT WARFARE between Hamas and Israel shatters two myths that have been accepted as gospel by many in the international community and the media.

Myth 1: The primary cause of the conflict between Israel and the Palestinians is the occupation of the West Bank and Israel's settlement policy.

Reality: The reality is that Hamas's rocket attacks against Israeli cities and civilian targets have little to do with Israel's occupation and settlement policy on the West Bank. Even if Israel were to make peace with the Palestinian Authority, the rocket attacks from Gaza would not stop. These Hamas attacks are incited by the Muslim Brotherhood, Iran, Syria, and others opposed to the very concept of the nation-state for the Jewish people. The best proof of this reality is that these attacks began as soon as Israel ended its occupation of Gaza and uprooted all the civilian settlements from that area. Israel left behind agricultural hothouses and other equipment that the residents of Gaza could have used to build a decent society.

Moreover, there was no siege of Gaza at that time. Gaza was free to become a Singapore on the Mediterranean. Instead, Hamas engaged in a coup d'état, murdering many members of the PA, seizing control of all of Gaza, and turning it into a militant theocracy. It used the material left behind by the Israelis not to feed its citizens but to build rockets with which to attack Israeli civilians. It was only after these rocket attacks that Israel began a siege of Gaza designed to prevent the importation of rockets and material used to build terrorist kidnap tunnels.

There are good reasons why Israel should change its settlement policy in the West Bank and try harder to achieve peace with the PA.

But even if that were to be accomplished, the rockets from Gaza would continue and Israel would have to take the kind of military steps any democracy would take to protect its civilians from lethal aggression.

Myth 2: Mahmoud Abbas is part of the solution, not part of the problem.

Reality: Mahmoud Abbas has become part of the problem. He has publicly supported Hamas in its war crimes against Israeli civilians and has characterized Israel's self-defense actions as "genocide" against all of the Palestinian people. I have met Abbas and found him to be a decent man who genuinely wants a peaceful solution to the conflict, but he is not a man of courage who is prepared to stand up and tell the Palestinian people the truth about the current conflict. His willingness to join together with Hamas in a governmental partnership demonstrates both his weakness and his willingness to be complicit with evil. He speaks out of two sides of his mouth, one side when he speaks in English to Western media and diplomats, and the other when he speaks in Arabic to the Palestinian street, which he knows contains many supporters of Hamas. His public support for Hamas has made it far more difficult for Israel to arrive at a negotiated solution with the PA. It has also made it more difficult for Hamas to stop the rocket barrage and agree to a cease-fire.

21

Israel Must Maintain
Its Weapons Siege of Gaza

July 14, 2014

W HENEVER the current conflict in Gaza ends, and whatever the terms of any cease-fire, Israel will have to maintain its weapons siege against Gaza.

The current conflict plainly revealed how inadequate the previous siege was. Thousands upon thousands of rockets, including long-range ones capable of hitting Tel Aviv, Jerusalem, and the West Bank, found their way into Gaza despite the siege that Israel began after the rocket fire that accompanied Israel's decision to end its military occupation of Gaza. Some of these rockets came from Iran, others from Syria, while still others were assembled in Gaza from material brought in from the outside.[1] These rockets place Israeli civilian lives in jeopardy, even if the Iron Dome has shown success in thwarting most of them.

1 See for example: Yaakov Lappin, "Syrian-made M302 Rocket Fired by Hamas at Hadera," *The Jerusalem Post*, 7 September 2014, and Dan Williams, "Israel Seizes Arms Shipment," *Reuters*, 5 March 2014.

There can be absolutely no doubt that a military blockade designed to prevent the importation of lethal aggressive weapons is entirely lawful under international law. Even a UN commission, not known for its partiality toward Israel, agreed that the naval blockade was entirely lawful.[2] Our own State Department concluded that such a blockade was lawful when the United States quarantined Cuba in a successful effort to keep the former Soviet Union from shipping nuclear missiles to its shores.

Any future quarantine should exclude food, medicine, and other necessities of life that do not pose a direct threat to Israeli security. But there must be a total quarantine on the importation of rockets and rocket parts. This includes the shutting down of the many smuggling tunnels between Egypt and Gaza, or at the very least, some reliable inspection of what is allowed to go through those tunnels. It obviously also includes a shutting down of *all* of the terrorist tunnels that now exist or are being built between Gaza and Israel proper. The only purpose of these tunnels is to allow Hamas to kidnap and/or kill Israelis and to bring them or their bodies back to Gaza to hold them in exchange for Hamas prisoners.

No country is required to accept such lethal threats to its citizens. The only other possible alternative to an enhanced military siege is for there to be *reliable* inspectors throughout Gaza whose job it is to prevent the rearming of Hamas. It is unlikely that Hamas would agree to any such inspectors. The experience in Lebanon, where Hezbollah has armed to the teeth right in front of United Nations inspectors, demonstrates how difficult this task would be even if Hamas agreed to some monitoring.

2 Geoffrey Palmer et al., "Report of the Secretary-General's Panel of Inquiry on the 31 May 2010 Flotilla Incident," September 2011: 4.

Israel made a serious mistake in ending the *military* occupation of Gaza. It was right to end the settlement project, which did not serve to enhance Israel's security. There is an enormous difference—in law, in morality, and in practicality—between a *military occupation* and *civilian settlements*. Under the laws of war, a military occupation may continue until the enemy has put down its arms and the risk to the other side has been eliminated or at least significantly diminished. Those conditions were not met when Israel ended its military occupation of Gaza back in 2005. Israel should have maintained a sufficient military force in Gaza to assure that thousands of rockets could not be built or fired from hostile territory.

It is probably too late now, and too costly, for Israel to reoccupy the Gaza Strip. A far less restrictive alternative is to enhance the military siege while eliminating any humanitarian siege. This will not be easy to accomplish, but it is far better than maintaining the current status quo whereby Hamas fires rockets at Israel, is attacked, achieves a cease-fire, rearms, attacks Israel again, and is attacked in turn. An ounce of weapons siege is worth a pound of rocket fire and air attacks.

Any siege of Gaza, even if it is limited to a weapons siege, will have a negative impact on the million and a half civilians who live in that densely populated area. But if the siege is limited to weapons, the impact will be far less than the inevitable deaths and injuries caused by Hamas firing rockets into Israel and Israel retaliating. Although the blame for these civilian deaths falls squarely on the shoulders of Hamas, because it is Hamas that fires its rockets from densely populated areas, it is the Palestinian civilians who pay the heavy price. They pay this heavy price because Hamas deliberately refuses to build shelters for its civilians. They do build shelters and tunnels to protect their terrorists, those who fire the rockets and other combatants. Hamas could easily fire its rockets from the many spacious areas outside of Gaza City. It could build military bases from which to wage warfare. But instead it has chosen this dead baby strategy, whereby it encourages or compels civilians to become human shields, precisely in order to display the dead babies, women, and disabled whom they know will be killed when Israel attacks their rockets.

A weapons siege imposes a heavy toll on the civilian population, but the toll would not be nearly as heavy as that imposed by the current Hamas strategy. The great tragedy is that Israel, like any democracy, is put to three tragic choices:

1. It could tolerate thousands of rockets being aimed at its civilians in the hope that the Iron Dome will prevent deaths and injuries;

2. It can respond to these rocket attacks by proportionate and targeted military strikes, as it is now doing; or

3. It can prevent the rearming of Hamas by a narrowly limited weapons siege.

The last of these alternatives is the least worst choice.

22

Media Death Count Encourages Hamas to Use Human Shields

July 15, 2014

T HE MEDIA LOVES to count the dead bodies on each side of a conflict. It's much easier to count than to explain. Hamas knows this. That's why they employ what I call the dead baby strategy.

Hamas's strategy since Israel left Gaza in 2005 has been exactly the same. The media response has been exactly the same. And Hamas will continue to employ a strategy that causes many Palestinian civilians to die as long as the media keeps up its thoughtless body count.

Hamas could easily reduce the death and injury toll among its civilians by simply allowing them to go underground into tunnels and shelters that abound throughout Gaza. But Hamas has a deliberate policy of refusing to allow civilians to enter the tunnels or shelters. They reserve these places of refuge for their fighters and commanders, which explains why so few Hamas fighters have been killed. If Hamas were to reverse its policy and allow civilians into the shelters while requiring its fighters to stay above ground, the ratio of civilians to fighters killed would dramatically change. That is why in each of the wars between Hamas and Israel there have been more Palestinian than Israeli civilian deaths and injuries. It is part of Hamas's dead baby strategy, and it works because the media facilitates it.

The media also emphasizes the fact that thus far no Israelis have been killed by Hamas rocket fire.[1] Indeed some media and international organizations seem implicitly to be condemning Israel for protecting the lives of its own citizens, by repeatedly pointing out that none have died while Palestinian deaths have reached nearly two hundred. The reason there have been no Israeli deaths so far is because Israel spends hundreds of millions of dollars trying to protect its civilians while Hamas spends its resources deliberately exposing its civilians to the risks of Israeli counterattacks. Israel has built shelters all throughout the country and has spent a fortune on the Iron Dome system. The results have been impressive, though many Israelis suffer from trauma, shock, and the inevitable long-term consequences of being exposed to constant rocket fire.

How many times have you heard, seen, or read the body counts: nearly two hundred Palestinians dead, no Israelis dead. This is usually accompanied by an accusation that Israel is violating the international law requirement of "proportionality." This is a misuse of the term, which has a precise meaning in international law that reflects a broader morality. Under international law, a nation has the right to attack military targets. Period! It doesn't matter whether the rockets coming from these launchers have as yet succeeded in their task of killing civilians. There can be no doubt under international law that rocket launchers, and the fighters who employ them, are legitimate military targets. Israel is therefore entitled to attack these targets, even if no Israeli civilians

---

1 Since that time, several Israeli civilians, including a four-year-old child, were killed by rockets from Gaza.

have been killed, so long as it can do so without causing disproportionate civilian casualties.

This rule was not addressed to an enemy that deliberately uses human shields to protect its military targets and combatants against legitimate attacks. Proportionality is not judged by the number of civilians actually killed by Hamas rockets, but rather by the risks posed to Israelis. These risks have been diminished but not eliminated by the Iron Dome system. They have also been considerably diminished by Israel's counterattacks on the missile launchers and those who employ them. Without these counterattacks, it is highly likely that more Hamas missiles would have made it through the Iron Dome system, which has been approximately 85 percent effective.[2] Israel has every right under the rules of proportionality to attack these military targets, so long as they take reasonable efforts to reduce civilian casualties. They have done so by leafleting, by calling, and by other methods of warning civilians to leave target areas. Hamas leaders, on the other hand, have urged, and sometimes compelled, their civilians to remain in harm's way as human shields.

The media, by emphasizing the comparative body counts without providing the reasons for the disparity, play into the hands of Hamas and encourage that terrorist organization to continue to pursue its dead baby strategy. So the next time those in the media promote a body count without explanation, they should point a finger at themselves for contributing to this deadly count.

2 "Iron Dome: How Israel's Missile Defence System Works," *The Week*, 1 August 2014.

23

Netanyahu,
the Reluctant Warrior

July 20, 2014

ENJAMIN NETANYAHU has said that the primary goal
of the current ground incursion into Gaza is to destroy the terror tunnels that endanger Israel's security.
It requires boots on the ground to get to these tunnels
and to shut them down. Nor does Israel yet have the techni-
cal capacity to determine the route of the tunnels and their
exit points since they are deep underground and not subject
to detection from the air.

The event that immediately provoked this ground incursion was the discovery by Israel of yet another tunnel—in
addition to the one I was in during June of 2014—whose
exit was near a civilian kibbutz. This discovery almost came
too late to prevent a mass casualty disaster. The terrorists had
already emerged from the tunnel with grenade launchers,
bazookas, machine guns and other weapons capable of mass
murder (http://www.haaretz.com/news/video/1.605650).
Several of the terrorists were killed while others apparently
escaped back through the tunnel before the Israelis could
disable it.

This attempted mass casualty attack was planned and

implemented while Israel and Egypt were trying to arrange a cease-fire. Israeli intelligence estimates that there are dozens of other terror tunnels that they still cannot find although they know where some of the entrance points in Gaza are located. It is these tunnels that are the primary object of Israel's risky ground incursion.

There are other tunnels as well on the west side of Gaza, underneath its border with Egypt. These are the smuggling tunnels through which Hamas imports the rockets that it uses to terrorize Israeli civilians. It also uses these tunnels to enrich its leaders, who take a percentage of the profits earned by the commerce that goes through these tunnels on a daily basis. These smuggling tunnels too pose a direct threat to Israel's security and are a secondary object of Israel's ground incursion.

The end result of Israel's military operation should be twofold: First, to stop the security threat currently posed by Hamas terrorism—rocket fire, kidnappings, and terrorist incursions into Israel—by shutting down the tunnels and imposing a strict quarantine against the importation of rockets and against the exportation of terrorists through tunnels; and second, to restore the flow of innocent commerce into Gaza so that its citizens can live lives as normal as possible while they remain under the thumb of the violent theocracy and kleptocracy of Hamas.

The Israeli government did not want to send troops into Gaza. Its leaders well understand the risks to their own soldiers as well as to Palestinian civilians. But they also understand the risks to Israeli civilians of allowing these terrorist tunnels to continue to operate underneath its border. The decision to send in troops was a difficult one, made on the basis of a calculation of the risks of action versus the risks of inaction.

Shortly after I went into the tunnel underneath the Gaza-Israel border, I had a private dinner with Prime Minister Netanyahu. It was clear to me how reluctant Netanyahu was to send troops into Gaza. He had never before committed ground troops into an enemy war zone. As is well known, his own brother was killed defending Israel against terrorism. He knows the price of action as well as inaction. He is a reluctant warrior, but Hamas forced his hand by repeatedly turning down negotiated cease-fires and continuing to fire rockets at Israeli cities and to send terrorists into Israeli kibbutzim. No democracy would have acted differently in the face of such dangers.

24

Gazans' Real Enemy
Is Hamas, Not Israel

July 20, 2014

WHEN ISRAEL ended its occupation of Gaza in 2005, it left behind farm equipment and other material capable of feeding the population. Donor countries promised support, financial and political, if Gaza would live up to its potential as a Singapore on the Mediterranean. But instead the leaders of Gaza enriched themselves and used the remaining resources to build rockets instead of ploughshares. They fired these rockets at Israeli civilians and devised a strategy of using their own innocent civilians as human shields against Israel's anticipated responses to the rocket fire. Only after Hamas started firing rockets at Israeli civilians did Israel impose a painful blockade against Gaza that contributed to the area's poor economic situation.

The Hamas human shield strategy—in combination with its refusal to allow its civilians to seek shelter in Gaza's many tunnels, which are reserved for Hamas terrorists and commanders—has resulted in what appears to be a disproportionate ratio of civilians to combatants among Gazan casualties. Although the international media blames this unfortunate ratio on Israel, the civilian population of Gaza knows the truth: that Hamas deliberately seeks to increase the number of civilian casualties by not providing them shelter, while seeking to decrease the number of terrorist casualties by providing them the safety of tunnels and other secure areas.

Following the publication of the *Goldstone Report* in 2009, which catalogued the high proportion of civilians to combatant deaths among Gazans, loud complaints were heard from many ordinary citizens of Gaza: Why do you protect Hamas fighters while exposing civilians? Hamas responded by claiming—quite ironically—that many of those counted as civilians by the *Goldstone Report*, especially among the police, were actually Hamas combatants.

Whatever the facts turn out to be during the present encounter, more and more Gazans are beginning to understand how ill served they have been by Hamas. And now media reports are documenting the extraordinary wealth accumulated by Hamas leaders at the expense of ordinary Gazans. As one report put it: "With multi-million-dollar land deals, luxury villas and black-market fuel from Egypt, Gaza's rulers made billions while the rest of the population struggled with 38 per cent poverty and 40 per cent unemployment."[1] The report went on to detail the newly acquired wealth of specific Hamas leaders, strongly suggesting that this violent theocracy has also become a criminal kleptocracy at the expense of the people of Gaza.

During a recent radio interview, I was asked what I would do if I were a resident of Gaza, suffering from unemployment and Israeli rocket counterattacks. My answer was simple: I would try to overthrow the Hamas regime and make a deal with Israel under which Gaza would give up

1 Doron Peskin, "Hamas got Rich as Gaza was Plunged into Poverty," *ynetnews.com*, 15 July 2014.

its rockets in exchange for a Marshall Plan that would feed and normalize its residents. Such a plan would require international inspection of imports and the end of the tunnel economy that has enriched Hamas leaders and allowed the importation of lethal rockets. The present Hamas leadership is unlikely to accept any plan that takes away its money and weapons, but if the people of Gaza were to demand change—a real "Gaza spring"—anything is possible.

Many years ago Golda Meir engaged in hyperbolic overgeneralization when she said that peace would come "when Palestinians love their children more than they hate Israel." Most Palestinians love their children. Many do hate Israel because they have been taught to hate for generations. But more and more of them are coming to realize that the real enemy is not Israel, which left the Gaza Strip in 2005 and offered to leave most of the West Bank in 2000, 2001, and 2008. The real enemies of the Palestinians are those Hamas leaders who do love Palestinian children less than they hate Israel. That's why they are prepared to use these children as human sacrifices in their efforts to destroy the nation-state of the Jewish people.

There will be peace between Israel and the Palestinians only when the Palestinians overthrow or vote out the violent theocrats and kleptocrats of Hamas—or when Hamas can be induced by the citizens of Gaza to change its destructive policies. The alternative will be a Gaza in which civilians continue to pay the heavy price for Hamas's hatred of Israel and contempt for its own citizens.

25

Why Doesn't J Street
Support Israel?

July 21, 2014

A NY PRETENSE that J Street is a pro-Israel organization
has been destroyed by that organization's refusal to
participate in a solidarity rally for Israel during the
recent crisis in Gaza.

The Boston Jewish Federation worked hard to create
a rally that included all elements of its diverse community.
Its goal was to send a single and simple message: at a time
when so many in the world are united against Israel's efforts
at defending itself from Hamas rockets and terrorist tunnels,
the Boston Jewish community stands in solidarity with the
nation-state of the Jewish people. In order to assure that this
message of unity was sent, no signs were permitted except
for the unity message that was intended to be sent. That
message was: Stand With Israel. Simple and straightforward.

Speakers were limited to those who were part of the
broad Jewish consensus including rabbis, political and business leaders, and the highly regarded head of the federation,
Barry Shrage, whose commitment to peace and the two-state
solution is well known.

Initially J Street agreed to be a cosponsor of this unity event, but then—presumably after receiving pressure from its hard-left constituency, which is always looking to bash Israel and never to support it—J Street was forced to withdraw its sponsorship. The phony excuse it offered was that the rally offered "no voice for [J Street] concerns about the loss of human life on both sides" and no recognition of the "complexity" of the issues or the need for a "political solution."

This is total nonsense and an insult to those who spoke at the rally. The executive director of the Jewish Community Relations Council spoke of the "suffering" of the people of Gaza and how "painful" it is "to see innocent people dying, including children."

Barry Shrage spoke of the "tragedy" of innocent Palestinians being killed. All the speakers acknowledged the "complexity" of the issues and want to see a political solution to the conflict. Yet J Street refused to be part of this unified show of support for Israel.

J Street has whined about being excluded from the mainstream Jewish community, but it is J Street that has excluded itself from joining in community activities such as this rally. It was J Street that decided not to participate in a unity event that was jointly sponsored by the Jewish Federation and the Jewish Community Relations Council.

J Street has sought and received membership in these sponsoring organizations but then made a decision to withdraw its own sponsorship from this community-wide event, precisely at a time when unity was most needed. J Street has always insisted on a double standard. On the one hand, it wants to be part of the Jewish community's Big Tent, but on the other hand, it refuses to allow dissenters into its own narrow, ideological tent. I know, because I have personally asked to speak to its members at its convention.

J Street has adamantly refused to allow its members to hear my centrist point of view—I support the two-state solution and oppose Israel's settlement policies—while welcoming extremist speakers who support boycotts of Israel and who refuse to recognize Israel as the nation-state of the Jewish people.

Its own tent flap is open only on the left side, not in the center. J Street's decision to refuse to sponsor this community-wide Stand With Israel rally during so critical a time has drawn a line in the sand. If you can't support Israel now, how can you call yourself a pro-Israel organization? How can any member of J Street now look at themselves in the mirror and say, "I belong to a pro-Israel organization"?

I call on members of J Street who are truly pro-Israel to leave that divisive organization and to join with us who truly support Israel during times of crisis while remaining critical of some of its policies. If you are pro-Israel, you do not belong in J Street, because J Street can no longer credibly claim to be pro-Israel.

If there was ever any doubt about that, J Street's actions in refusing to join the Stand With Israel rally should resolve them. So if you want to stand with Israel, stand up against J Street and stand with organizations that support Israel during times of crisis.

26

Hamas's Threat to Israel's Airport Threatens a Two-State Solution

July 22, 2014

Hamas's decision to fire rockets in the direction of Ben-Gurion Airport may well have ended any real prospect of a two-state solution. Whether the regulators and airlines that have stopped flights to and from Israel[1] are right or wrong, this stoppage cannot possibly be tolerated by a democratic country that relies so heavily on tourism and international travel. It is, of course, a war crime to target an international civilian airport, as Hamas admits it has done. Israel has every right to keep that airport open, employing all reasonable military means at its disposal. Since Hamas fires its rockets from densely populated civilian areas, there will be more Palestinian civilian deaths.

This of course is part of Hamas's grand strategy: by targeting Israeli civilians and international air travel from its own civilian areas, Hamas leaves Israel no choice but to take

---

1 Zohar Blumenkrantz, "Airlines Suspend Israel Flights over Missile Fears," *Haaretz*, 22 July 2014.

military actions that risk the lives of innocent Palestinians. There will be even more innocent Palestinian deaths now, as Hamas has raised the stakes considerably for Israel. Every country in the world would do everything in its power to keep open its airports, the lifelines to its economic viability. Hamas knows this—and welcomes Israeli military action that produces more dead Palestinian civilians and hence more international criticism of Israel.

Even more importantly, Hamas's actions in essentially closing down international air traffic into Israel considerably reduce the prospect of any two-state solution. Israel will now be more reluctant than ever to give up military control over the West Bank, which is even closer to Ben-Gurion Airport than is Gaza.

Were Israel to end its military occupation of the West Bank—as distinguished from its civilian settlements deep in the West Bank—it would risk the possibility of a Hamas takeover. That is precisely what happened when Israel ended both its civilian settlements and its military presence in Gaza. Hamas took control, fired thousands of rockets at Israeli civilian targets, and have now succeeded in stopping international air traffic into and out of Israel.

Israel could not accept the risk of a Hamas takeover of the West Bank and the resulting Hamas rocket attacks at its nearby airport. It may still be possible to create a two-state solution whereby Israel withdraws its civilian settlers from most of the West Bank and agrees to land swaps for areas that now contain large settlement blocks. But Israel will have to retain military control over its security borders, which extend to the Jordan River. It will also have to maintain a sufficient military presence to assure that what happened in Gaza does not happen in the West Bank. These military realities do not have to exist forever. Israel's military presence could be reduced if the Palestinian Authority were to maintain effective control over the West Bank and prevent terrorists from using that area to send rockets and terrorists into Israel.

The new reality caused by Hamas shutting down international air travel to and from Israel would plainly justify an Israeli demand that it maintain military control over the West Bank in any two-state deal. The Israeli public would never accept a deal that did not include a continued Israeli military presence in the West Bank. They have learned the tragic lesson of Gaza, and they will not allow it to be repeated on the West Bank. The Palestinian Authority, however, is unlikely to accept such a condition, though it should. This will simply make it far more difficult for an agreement to be reached.

It was precisely one of the goals of the Hamas rocket and tunnel assaults to scuttle any two-state agreement between the Palestinian Authority and Israel. The Hamas Charter categorically rejects the two-state solution, as does the military wing of Hamas. In this tragic respect, Hamas has already succeeded. By aiming its rockets in the direction of Ben-Gurion Airport, Hamas may well have scuttled any realistic prospects for a two-state solution. It cannot be allowed to succeed.

The international community, which has a significant stake in protecting international air traffic from terrorist rocket attacks, must support Israel's efforts to stop these attacks—permanently. If Hamas is allowed to shut down Israel's major airport, every terrorist group in the world will begin to target airports throughout the world. The shooting down of the Malaysian airliner over the Ukraine will be but one of many such tragedies if Hamas is allowed to succeed. An attack on the safety of Israel's airport is an attack on the safety of all international aviation. Israel is the canary in the mine. What Hamas has done to Israeli aviation is a warning to the world. In its efforts to prevent Hamas from firing rockets at Ben-Gurion Airport, Israel is fighting for the entire civilized world against those who would shoot down civilian airliners. The world should support Israel in this noble fight, and in the process help preserve any realistic chance for a two-state solution.

27

Accusing Hamas of Using Human Shields Is Not Racist

July 23, 2014

WHILE ISRAEL USES SHELTERS and the Iron Dome to protect its civilians, Hamas uses its civilians to protect its rockets and its terrorists. Recently, supporters of Hamas have argued that to say that Hamas uses civilians as human shields is a manifestation of racism and an attempt to dehumanize Palestinians.

But it is Hamas's own leaders who have long boasted of this tragic reality. Listen to Fathi Hammad, a Hamas member of the Palestinian Legislative Council:

"For the Palestinian people, death has become an industry... This is why they have formed human shields of the women, the children, the elderly, and the mujahedeen, in order to challenge the Zionist bombing machine."

And listen to recent commentary by Magdi Khalil, an Egyptian-American, on Al-Jazeera:

Is it moral to launch missiles from hospitals, from schools, from bedrooms, from mosques, and from the roof of a church, where thousands of Gazans had found refuge? The church's priest was interviewed on CBN and said: "From the roof of this church, Hamas members are launching missiles at Israel. We welcomed them in our church, but they began launching missiles at Israel from the roof." Is this the moral high ground that my colleague is talking about?

Is it moral for Hamas leaders to hide in Al-Shifa Hospital, thus risking the lives of regular people? Is this the moral high ground? They are fleeing like rats, hiding behind patients in Gaza hospitals. Is it moral for Hamas leaders to hide behind these patients?

They garner sympathy over the corpses of children. This is part of the strategy of the Islamists. They consider sympathy garnered over the corpses of children to be a victory…

The whole world knows that Hamas does not care about the spirit of humanity. They do not care about the children, about their people, about the losses, about the destruction of their country, or about the number of casualties.

We are talking about a group like ISIS. What kind of honor is it if it is at the expense of children's corpses? You don't know the meaning of life. All you know is the meaning of death. You constitute an enterprise of destruction in the region. You are wreaking destruction in Palestine. You don't know the meaning of life.

Go and die, brother, but don't make others die instead. If you want to die—go and die. Let Khaled Mash'al die. Let Haniya and Al-Zahhar die. Just don't let the children die.[1]

1 See http://www.memritv.org/clip_transcript/en/4441.htm.

Ban-Ki Moon—who is not known for a pro-Israel bias—recently confirmed what every objective observer knows to be true: that Hamas uses hospitals and schools as shields from which to launch rocket attacks against Israeli civilians—a double war crime. Here are his words:

"We condemn the use of civilian sites—schools, hospitals, and other civilian facilities—for military purposes."

He was referring, of course, to Hamas, since Israel does not use such civilian facilities to fire rockets. That is why more Palestinians than Israelis have died in recent weeks.

During a two-day period while dozens of Palestinians and several Israelis were killed, the media failed to report that in neighboring Syria, 700 Arabs and Muslims were killed in two days of fighting. This constitutes only a tiny fraction of the 160,000 people killed in Syria during the ongoing civil war. According to the Britain-based Syrian Observatory for Human Rights, 53,978 civilians have been killed, including 8,607 children and 5,586 women. Many if not most of these deaths were deliberate—part of calculated efforts on both sides of the conflict to maximize civilian casualties. Yet this body count has received little notice compared to the far smaller body count in Israel and Gaza. Why is this?

Is it because when Arabs and Muslims deliberately kill other Arabs and Muslims, that deserves less attention than when Israelis kill Arabs and Muslims, even in self-defense and in an effort to prevent the murder of their own civilians?

If so, this is racism pure and simple and the application of a noxious double standard. The lives of all human beings have worth, and the death of Arabs and Muslims at the hands of other Arabs and Muslims deserve as much media coverage as the deaths of Arabs and Muslims that are caused by Israel's efforts to protect its own civilians.

The media's exclusive focus on the death toll in Gaza—without explaining that it is largely Hamas's fault and part of its media strategy—incites hatred and anti-Semitism around the world. It has incited violence against Jews and Jewish institutions in many cities. Much of this violence comes from radicals on the hard left and from radical Islamists. But a recent incident in Italy shows that bigoted hate can come from the mouths of intellectuals as well as the fists of rabble-rousers.

Gianni Vattimo, who has been called Italy's most famous philosopher, recently announced that he would personally "like to shoot those bastard Zionists," calling them "a bit worse than the Nazis." He said he was planning to launch a fund-raising campaign to buy better rockets for Hamas so that this Jew-hating group can kill more Zionists, by which he means Jewish Israelis.

He urged European volunteers to join Hamas and fight alongside of them against Israel, as volunteers fought against Franco during the Spanish Civil War. If Vattimo is indeed Italy's most famous philosopher, I cry for the current state of philosophy in a nation that has contributed so much to that field over the millennia.

Vattimo reminds me of the intellectual thugs—some of them eminent philosophers—who provided academic cover and justification for the fascist abuses of Hitler and Mussolini. It is interesting, and perhaps relevant, that Vattimo is a follower of Martin Heidegger, a philosopher who joined the Nazi Party and provided cover for its anti-Semitic policies.

Hamas, after all, is an outgrowth of the Muslim Brotherhood, which Heidegger actively supported during World War II. It is also interesting that Vattimo, who vociferously supports gay rights, would have such hatred for the one country in the Middle East that accords equal rights to gays and be so supportive of Hamas which punishes gays by torture and execution.

I challenge Gianni Vattimo to go to Gaza, where he

would surely be welcomed with open arms because of his support for Hamas. Once in Gaza, I challenge him to conduct a rally in support of gay rights, to hold up a sign supporting gay rights, to urge Gazans to sign a petition demanding equality for gays.

In Italy, Gianni Vattimo is openly gay and proud of it. He has described himself as a "gay, Communist Catholic." I challenge him to travel to Gaza with a partner and to declare that he intends to practice his right to be treated equally and fairly with his partner.

We all know what would happen to Vattimo if he engaged in any such freedom of speech or action. He would be tortured and killed by Hamas.

If Vattimo is afraid to travel to Gaza now, let him go to Iran. He was an admirer of Mahmoud Ahmadinejad and continues to support the Iranian policy of "making the state of Israel disappear from the map." Were he to visit the country he admires so much, and were he to publicly proclaim his sexual orientation, he would be hanged from one of the building cranes that the mullahs use to make sure that Ahmadinejad's notorious statement—that "there are no gays in Iran"—becomes true. He would also be attacked if he were to advocate Communism, Catholicism, or any "ism" other than anti-Zionism.

Were he to travel to Israel, on the other hand, he would be free to openly support Hamas and to advocate and practice his sexual preference. He would also be free to support Communism, practice Catholicism, or advocate anti-Zionism.

In one respect, and perhaps in one respect only, Hamas-controlled Gaza, mullah-controlled Iran, and democratic Israel are exactly the same: in all three countries, everyone is free to condemn Israel and to support Hamas.

Why then would a so-called intellectual—and a

self-proclaimed leftist—himself support, and urge others to help, a murderous terrorist group whose roots are in Nazi fascism and whose policies deny equality to women, gays, Christians, atheists, and dissenters. Is it because he loves Hamas, or because he hates the nation-state of the Jewish people so much that he is prepared to close his eyes to the abuses of the terrorist group he supports?

The answer seems clear. Gianni Vattimo does not deserve the noble title of philosopher. He should be called by what he is: a hatemonger who applies a different standard in judging Hamas, Iran, and Israel.

Recently, Vattimo apologized to an Israeli newspaper (*Haaretz*) for saying he wished more Israelis were dying, claiming he was "provoked" by the hosts of the show on which he made his comments, but he repeated his comparison of Israel to Nazi Germany and maintained his view that Europe should provide more lethal weapons to Hamas, which would, of course, result in more Israeli civilians dying.

I urge Gianni Vattimo to accept my challenge and visit Gaza and/or Iran, rather than continuing to preach hatred of Israel and support for Hamas from the safety of Italy.

28

UN Probe of Israel Will Only Encourage Hamas War Crimes

July 24, 2014

"THERE YOU GO AGAIN," as Ronald Reagan said to Jimmy Carter. Once again the United Nations Human Rights Council has voted—with the United States dissenting—to conduct a so-called investigation of Israel's military responses to Hamas's double war crimes. Once again Israel will have to decide whether to feed the kangaroos that make up this court by cooperating with yet another phony investigation whose outcome is predetermined.

Yet again Israel is presented with a Hobson's choice: if it refuses to cooperate, it will be blamed for denying the investigatory commission relevant information; if it cooperates, it will lend credibility to a conclusion that has already been reached.

This Hamas-inspired investigation is an important part of Hamas's double war crime strategy: By firing its rockets from civilian areas and buildings—even Ban Ki-moon acknowledges that it does—Hamas seeks to have Israel kill as many Palestinian civilians as possible. This Hamas-designed body count, and the accompanying photographs, inevitably leads to the kind of one-sided investigation in which the UNHRC specializes.

The resulting one-sided condemnation, which Hamas can always count on, then helps it win support in Europe, South America, and other parts of the world, as well as in the media and universities.

By joining in this Hamas strategy, indeed becoming a central part of it, the UNHRC encourages Hamas to repeat its rocket fire against Israeli civilians, its tunneling into Israel to kill and kidnap Israelis, and its placement of its rockets and tunnel entrances in civilian areas. The countries voting for this investigation are fully aware of what they are encouraging. They have the blood of future innocent Palestinians and Israelis on their hands.

Last time around the commission found a willing dupe in Richard Goldstone, who was prepared to put his personal ambition to elevate his status within the international community above any commitment to truth. Because Goldstone is Jewish and has spent time in Israel, his name attached to the commission's report gave it an air of credibility. His dual conclusions—that Israel deliberately targeted Palestinian civilians and that Hamas did not use human shields—were so thoroughly discredited that they destroyed Goldstone's career and even his prospects of elevation within the international community. Eventually even Goldstone had to acknowledge his mistake and indicate that there was no evidentiary support for his widely cited conclusions.

This time around it will not be easy for the commission to find an ambitious dupe like Goldstone, because potential commission members now understand that their conclusions, methodologies, and biases will be scrutinized with care and exposed for all to read.

The council will probably have to satisfy itself with a group of overtly anti-Israel zealots who don't care about their reputations and who are willing to go through the motions of an investigation and come to the conclusion that the commission has anointed them to reach.

This process has already begun with the appointment of William Schabas, a known Israel-hater, as the chairman of the inquiry commission. Even before reviewing any evidence, Mr. Schabas declared that Israeli Prime Minister Benjamin Netanyahu should be tried as a war criminal. Indeed Mr. Schabas has espoused this position since 2011, the same year he cosponsored conferences at a Tehran-based "human rights" center that accuses Israel of the crime of apartheid, and which at the time was led by Mahmoud Ahmadinejad. He has also called for the International Criminal Court to prosecute president Shimon Peres, comparing him to Omar al-Bashir, the president of Sudan who has been indicted for directing the campaign of mass killings in Darfur.[1]

It would be useful to have a real investigation of both sides to the conflict conducted by objective experts. I would welcome such an investigation, as I suspect Israel would.

Objective investigators would seek hard evidence, such as real-time videos, communications within the military, forensic evidence, and other information that would allow open-minded investigators to find the facts wherever the facts take them. The problem is Hamas would never consent to such an investigation and would refuse to allow objective investigators into Gaza.

Indeed, the best proof of the pro-Hamas bias of any investigation is the fact that Hamas, which rules Gaza with an iron fist, would welcome these phony investigators with open arms, the way it welcomed Goldstone and his biased colleagues.

1 Yitzhak Benhorin, "Head of UN Gaza Inquiry Commission Called to Try Netanyahu at ICC," *Israel News*, 12 August 2014.

Despite the unwillingness of Hamas to allow objective investigators into Gaza, the world should demand a full and unbiased investigation by experienced, professional investigators, unconnected to the United Nations, whose sole responsibility should be to get at the truth, no matter how complex and nuanced it may turn out to be.

Such an independent, real investigation could be conducted at the same time that the phony UNHRC investigation is being conducted. Then the world would have a sound basis on which to compare the methodologies, factual findings, and conclusions of the two investigations. It would also have a sound basis on which to compare Hamas's actions with Israel's—and Israel's to what other democratic countries have done and would do when faced with comparable situations.

Any such investigation would also apply the rules of proportionality to the facts it found concerning Israel's military actions.

Even Navi Pillay, who runs the UNHRC, has acknowledged that proportionality permits a nation that has been attacked to counterattack enemy military targets so long as the military value of the target is important enough to justify the anticipated civilian casualties. This rule was not designed for situations in which the enemy deliberately uses civilians to shield its military operations.

In any event, the targets Israel has attacked—rockets aimed at civilians and terrorist tunnels built to kill and kidnap Israelis—are extremely important military targets that should not be immunized against counterattacks by deliberate use of human shields. Were the UNHRC to rule that the presence of human shields precludes a democracy from counterattacking important military targets—even after warning the civilians, as Israel does—this would encourage the widespread use of human shields by all terrorist groups around the world and put democracies at great peril.

But the UNHRC is likely to ignore that point, as it did in the *Goldstone Report*, and simply respond as Ms. Pillay has already responded, with the following cliché: "The actions of one party do not absolve the other party of the need to respect its obligations under international law."

This cliché—which is wrong, as a matter of both law and common sense, when the offending party deliberately uses human shields—is an invitation to Hamas and other terrorist groups to continue its double war crimes.

Israel should have nothing to fear from an objective investigation. It should also have nothing to fear from the UNHRC investigation—if its biases are exposed for all to see.

29

The "Occupation of Gaza" Canard

July 30, 2014

ENEMIES OF ISRAEL who are seeking to justify Hamas rocket and tunnel attacks against Israeli civilians are mendaciously claiming that Israel has continued to occupy the Gaza Strip, even after its soldiers and settlers left the Strip in 2005. They claim that because Gaza was unlawfully still occupied, despite the absence of Israeli soldiers, resistance to the occupation—including the murder of Israeli civilians—is justified as a matter of international law. This claim is wrong for several independent reasons.

First, it is never justified to target and murder enemy civilians. Even if Israel did have a military occupation, as it does in the West Bank, it would still be a double war crime to fire rockets at Israeli civilians, using Palestinian civilians as human shields.

It would also be a war crime to murder or kidnap Israeli civilians. The only legitimate resistance to occupation is to target the soldiers who enforce the occupation.

Second, a military occupation of Gaza—as distinguished from civilian settlements—would be entirely justified, both as a matter of law and common sense, because Hamas, which controls Gaza, is at war with Israel and has repeatedly refused to make peace with the nation-state of the Jewish people. A military occupation is proper as long as a state of war exists.

Third, and even more important for any future peace, is the indisputable fact that Israel, in fact, ended its occupation of Gaza in 2005.

The years between 2005 and the present must be divided into three time periods: 2005 to 2007; 2007 to the beginning of July 2014; and the beginning of July 2014 to the present.

During the first period (2005 to 2007), Israel removed all of its troops from Gaza.

It also removed all of its settlers.

The settlers left behind greenhouses, farm equipment and other valuable civilian assets worth millions of dollars.[1]

The Palestinians of Gaza were free to come and go as they pleased, to conduct free elections, and to import construction and other economic material in order to build a viable Palestinian entity to help their citizens. European donors sent them money and other resources, hoping that they would use them to create jobs, schools, hospitals and other necessary infrastructure.

To be sure, Israel maintained control over its border with Gaza, with checkpoints and security fences, but it opened its border to Palestinian residents of Gaza who came to work in Israel. During that period, numerous Gazans came into Israel to work and came back to Gaza with good salaries to feed their families.

During the same period many Gazans went to Egypt and other countries.

Israel continued to control Gaza's air space and to patrol its sea lanes in order to prevent the importation of rockets

---

1 "Looters Strip Gaza Greenhouses," *The Associated Press*, 13 September 2005.

and other weapons capable of being used against Israeli civilians, but it had no presence on the ground in Gaza.

On January 25, 2006, the Palestinian Authority held elections. Gazans were free to vote and did in fact vote in large numbers for Hamas, which achieved a significant political victory. But that wasn't enough for Hamas, which conducted a bloody coup d'état in which numerous Palestinian civilians who were associated with the Palestinian Authority were killed.

Hamas also resumed rocket attacks against Israeli civilians and increased its building of terrorist tunnels into Israel, which it used to kill and kidnap Israelis. It was only after these acts of war by Hamas that Israel instituted its blockade in 2007—nearly two years after it ended its occupation.

So the truth is that the blockade has not been the cause of Hamas's rocket and tunnel attacks. The blockade has been the result of these attacks. It is an entirely legitimate defensive military response to war crimes committed by Hamas.

Yet there are some—including Mark Lamont Hill and Peter Beinart, with whom I debated on CNN—who insist that Israel continued to "occupy" Gaza unlawfully between 2005 and 2007, before it instituted its blockade.

It's this kind of rigid, unnuanced argument that makes a compromise peace so difficult.

Finally, we come to the recent war. Israel did not send soldiers into Gaza until after Hamas sent its terrorists into Israel through its tunnels to kill Israelis. It became clear to Israel that it could not tolerate these tunnels, whose exits are located near kindergartens, kibbutzim, and other civilian areas. Nor could these tunnels be attacked from the air, since their entrances are beneath hospitals, schools, mosques, and civilian homes—and their exit locations are unknown to the Israelis.

The only way to shut down these terror tunnels is by

Israeli boots on the ground, and with grave risks to the lives of Israeli soldiers. But Israel had little choice but to attack these tunnel entrances before they could be used as planned: to murder hundreds, if not thousands of Israeli civilians and to kidnap Israeli soldiers and civilians.

Despite these indisputable realities, Israel's defamers insist that: 1) Gaza has been continuously occupied since its soldiers and settlers left in 2005; 2) Israel's continued occupation is unlawful; and 3) this unlawful occupation justifies Hamas's war crimes, including rocket and tunnel attacks on Israel's civilians from behind Palestinian human shields.

If any of these claims were to be credited by the international community, a two-state solution would become impossible, because there is no way Israel would, or should, end its military occupation of the West Bank without maintaining some degree of military control over its security borders. No Israeli government—right, left or center—would make a deal with the Palestinian Authority that left its citizens and its airport vulnerable to rocket or tunnel attacks of the kind they have experienced from Gaza since leaving in 2005. Nor would, or should, the United States ever ask Israel to accept any deal that did not assure its security, especially in light of the instability in Syria, Iraq, and much of the rest of the Arab and Muslim world.

Those who refuse to credit Israel for unilaterally removing all of its settlers and all of its soldiers from Gaza because it retained some security control over its borders are discouraging Israel from taking further risks for peace.

The perfect is enemy of the good, and to demand a total end to any Israeli military control over its vulnerable and dangerous borders is to assure that a good, if imperfect, peace deal will never take place. That is the goal of Hamas. It is also the goal of some Israeli extremists.

Those who falsely argue that Israel continued to occupy Gaza after its soldiers left and before it imposed its necessary blockade are playing into the hands of the enemies of a compromise peace.

30

Qatar and Other
American "Allies" Are
Among the Villains in Gaza

August 1, 2014

AMERICAN ALLIES, especially Qatar and Turkey, have been providing material support to Hamas, which the United States has listed as a foreign terrorist organization. This support includes financial, diplomatic, media, and even the provision of weapons that deliberately target Israeli civilians from behind Palestinian civilians who are used as human shields. It also includes harboring war criminals, especially leaders of Hamas, who direct their followers from the safety of Doha. Without the support of Qatar and Turkey, Hamas would never have started this bloody war that has caused so much human suffering.

Qatar, which is more of a family-owned gas station than a real country, regards itself as untouchable because of its oil wealth. Its residents—they are not really citizens because there are no genuine elections or freedom of speech or religion—are the richest in the world. It can buy anything it wants, including the 2022 World Cup, several American university campuses, some of the world's greatest art, Al Jazeera television, and other luxuries. It can also buy terrorist groups such as Hamas. Indeed, after Iran, which is the world's worst state sponsor of terrorism, Qatar ranks near the top of this dishonor role of death.

Any individual who provides material support to a designated terrorist group such as Hamas commits a crime under the United States penal law and the laws of several European countries. If Hamas were ever to be convicted of war crimes by the International Criminal Court, as it may well be, any individual who was an accessory to such crimes would be guilty as well. It is entirely fair, therefore, to describe Qatar as a criminal regime, guilty of accessory to mass murder.

In some ways Turkey is even worse. Its erratic prime minister, Recep Tayyip Erdogan, has incited anti-Semitism, provoked conflict with Israel, provided material support to Hamas, and undercut efforts to achieve a realistic end to the Gaza War. He has demanded that his Jewish subjects do his bidding, telling "our Jewish citizens' leaders" that they must "adopt a firm stance and release a statement against the Israeli government." He has suggested that if they fail to do so they will not be regarded as "good Turks," thus raising the old canard of "dual loyalty."

Erdogan also recently said of Israel that "they always curse Hitler, but they now even exceed him in barbarism." And he responded to Americans who complain about the "comparisons with Hitler," by saying, "You're American, what's Hitler got to do with you?" forgetting that Hitler's forces killed thousands of American soldiers and civilians. He also conveniently forgets that Turkey, which remained immorally "neutral" in the war against Nazism, provided Hitler with the playbook for his genocide, by its own genocide against Armenians. As Hitler asked rhetorically when planning his genocide: "Who, after all, speaks today of the annihilation of the Armenians?" So Hitler matters to

America, as it should to Turkey, which still mendaciously denies that it committed genocide against the Armenians. Recently, the *New York Times* reported that Qatar was trying to buy the Brookings Institution and other Washington Think Tanks.[1]

Yet it was Qatar and Turkey to which Secretary of State John Kerry turned in his efforts to get Israel and Hamas to agree to a cease-fire. This not only infuriated Israel, which considers these two countries as accessories to Hamas's war crimes, but also Jordan, Egypt, and the Palestinian Authority, which also see Qatar and Turkey as allies of Hamas and enemies of moderate Arab states.

The time has come for the United States and the international community to reassess the status of Qatar and Turkey. These two countries have become part of the problem, rather than part of the solution. A nation that hosts Hamas leaders and finances their terrorism should not also host the World Cup. Nor should American universities send their faculty and students to a nation complicit in terrorism that has taken the lives of many Americans as well as Israelis.

Turkey's role in NATO must also be reevaluated. Membership in this organization entails certain responsibilities, and Turkey has failed in these responsibilities. They have become untrustworthy partners in the quest for peace.

It is a truism that we, as a nation, must deal with devils, because men and women are not angels. I do not fault Secretary of State Kerry for trying to use Qatar and Turkey to pressure Hamas into accepting a deal, although the deal

---

1 Eric Lipton, Brooke Williams, and Nicholas Confessore, "Foreign Powers Buy Influence at Think Tanks," the *New York Times*, 6 September 2014. It quoted the Qatar Ministry of Foreign Affairs as boasting that Brookings "will assume its role in reflecting the bright image of Qatar in the international media, especially the American ones."

they ultimately came up with was a bad one, especially compared to the Egyptian proposal. My point is that Qatar's wealth and Turkey's size should not preclude us from telling it as it is: Qatar and Turkey are among the worst villains in the Gaza tragedy. Nor should we reward such villains, and such complicity in war crimes, by international gifts, such as the World Cup. Both Qatar and Turkey should be treated as pariahs unless and until they stop becoming state sponsors, supporters, and facilitators of terrorism.

31

Hamas Uses Cease-Fire
to Kidnap

August 1, 2014

WHEN HAMAS ACCEPTED the US-UN proposed cease-fire, many eyebrows were raised.

Why suddenly would Hamas accept this cease-fire, when it had turned down so many previous proposals?

Some speculated that perhaps Qatar, the financial godfather of the terrorist organization, had pressured Hamas into accepting it. Others speculated that Hamas was getting pressure from its own citizens to end the bloodshed.

It now seems that all these speculations failed to take into account the true nature of Hamas. We often forget that Hamas is a criminal organization—a group of terrorists working together with other terrorist groups such as Islamic Jihad for the sole purpose of destroying the nation-state of the Jewish people and killing as many of its citizens as possible.

Criminals and terrorists don't play by the rules of civilized society.

It now seems likely that Hamas and its co-conspirators agreed to the deal for the sole purpose of lulling Israel into accepting it so that they could catch Israel off guard and exploit the humanitarian cease-fire to achieve one of the most important goals of the war they started, namely to kidnap an Israeli soldier or civilian and hold that person hostage until their extortionate demands were met.

The reason some people actually believed that Hamas would play by the rules and maintain the cease-fire to which it agreed, is because the media, the UN, and some in the international community falsely equate Israel, a democratic country that abides by the rule of law, with Hamas, a terrorist organization comprised of criminals who commit double war crimes every time they fire rockets at Israeli civilians from behind Palestinian civilians and whenever they hide terrorist tunnels in civilian areas.

The conflict is seen not as one between good and evil, or between criminals and those who seek to enforce the law, but rather as between two parties with equal claims. This false symmetry only encourages Hamas to exploit this status by appearing to play by the rules while never intending to do so.

Israel has learned its harsh lesson.

It will never again agree to a cease-fire with Hamas that in any way depends on mutual trust. One hopes that the world too has learned a lesson. It should never try to pressure Israel into taking any action or inaction that relies on Hamas's good faith.

Since it was the United States and United Nations that asked Israel to accept the cease-fire that led to the apparent kidnapping of an Israeli soldier, it is now their responsibility to demand the return of the soldier with no conditions.[1]

The United States has accepted this responsibility.

---

1 The IDF has since determined that the soldier was killed. His body, or parts of it, may have been taken by Hamas terrorists.

Secretary of State John Kerry issued the following statement: "The United States condemns in the strongest possible terms today's attack, which led to the killing of two Israeli soldiers and the apparent abduction of another... Hamas, which has security control over the Gaza Strip, must immediately and unconditionally release the missing Israeli soldier, and I call on those with influence over Hamas to reinforce this message."

The United Nations, on the other hand, has accepted no responsibility.

Its Security Council is unlikely to demand the unconditional and immediate return of the soldier or even condemn Hamas alone for violating the UN-brokered cease-fire. That is because Russia will almost certainly veto any unilateral condemnation of Hamas even if a majority could be mustered in support.

The best proof, if any were needed, that Hamas is a criminal organization, is that it regards the kidnapped soldier not as a prisoner of war but as a hostage. Responsible armed forces capture soldiers; criminal organizations kidnap them. Responsible armed forces allow the Red Cross to visit captured soldiers; criminal organizations keep them incommunicado and allow no Red Cross visitors.

Real armed forces release soldiers when the combat is over; criminal groups hold their kidnap victims until their ransom demands are met.

Finally, real armed forces protect the lives of captured enemy soldiers; criminal gangs often murder their kidnap victims, as Hamas members murdered the three Israeli children they kidnapped earlier this year.

The time has come, indeed it has long past, for the international community to regard Hamas as the terrorist gang that it is. It should be treated the way the world has treated pirates over the centuries. International warrants should be issued for the arrest of Hamas's gang leaders.

They should be dealt with in the way police and armed forces deal with the mafia and other criminal gangs. Hamas deserves no place at the table of negotiation or in any Palestinian government, any more than La Cosa Nostra would deserve to be part of an Italian government or the Israeli-Russian mafia should be included in any Israeli government.

Hamas has done more harm to the Palestinian people than has Israel. If the Palestinian people won't rescue themselves from this gang of cutthroats, the international community should do so.

That would be true humanitarianism.

32

What Should Israel Do?
What Would the United States Do?

August 5, 2014

I MAGINE YOU ARE the prime minister of Israel or the
president of the United States, or the chief of staff of
either army. Your soldiers are fighting a just war to try to
prevent rockets from hitting your civilians or tunnels from
being used to murder and kidnap your people. Your enemy,
knowing that you wish to prevent casualties among their civilians, purposely shoots at your soldiers from civilian areas.
Your soldiers, caught in the midst of an ongoing firefight,
basically have two choices: one, fire back and try to stop the
enemy from killing you while trying to avoid or minimize
civilian casualties; or two, lay down your arms because you
don't want to endanger civilians, and accept the risk that
your soldiers may be killed.

The United Nations and much of the rest of the world—
sitting in the safety of peaceful areas—have condemned
Israel for allowing its soldiers to try to stop the attacks on
them while also trying to minimize civilian casualties. "You
can do more," the White House has insisted.

But what more could Israel do that would not endanger
its own civilians and soldiers? Would President Obama like

to be the one who has to call the parents of an American soldier and explain to them that their son was killed because he, the commander in chief, had ordered the soldier not to fire back at enemy mortars that were being fired at him from behind human shields?

Israel is doing precisely what every other Western democracy would do if confronted with the situation Israel now faces. Colonel Richard Kemp—a British expert on this kind of warfare—has said that Israel is doing it more carefully and with more concern for civilian life than any other country. The Israeli military devotes considerable resources to trying to minimize Palestinian civilian casualties, while Hamas devotes its resources to trying to maximize both Israeli and Palestinian civilian casualties.

It is worth remembering what the United States and Great Britain did during the Second World War. After German rockets were fired at London, Winston Churchill ordered the carpet bombing of Dresden, deliberately intending to kill as many civilians—men, women, and children—as possible in order to weaken the morale of his enemy. The United States firebombed Tokyo, killing one hundred thousand people, and then dropped two nuclear bombs, killing many more. The United States has also killed many civilians in Afghanistan, Iraq, and Kosovo, as have Great Britain and other members of NATO. In none of these wars did Western armies take the precautions and give the warnings that Israel has undertaken.

It is unseemly and hypocritical for the Western world to castigate Israel for doing exactly what it would do and has done when faced with comparable or even less serious threats.

In Israel, these moral issues are debated endlessly, among philosophers, in the media, within the military, by politicians, and by the general public. There are no easy answers, except to those sitting the safety of Washington DC, Turtle Bay, London, and Paris. For Israelis, the questions are real, involving life-and-death decisions. How should the democratic nation balance the lives of its own civilians and soldiers against risks to the lives of enemy civilians? Those who condemn Israel in simplistic terms should try to address some of these more nuanced questions. A reasonable moralist might answer these questions differently than Israel and other democracies have, but Israel's answers are well within the rules of engagement employed by the United States, NATO, and even the United Nations.

President Obama has recognized the difficulties faced by Israel in protecting its citizens from rockets and terror tunnels that are deliberately placed in hospitals, United Nations facilities, mosques, and civilian homes. It is part of Hamas's strategy to place these lethal weapons in densely populated areas, precisely in order to maximize Palestinian civilian casualties.

Israeli soldiers and civilians should not have to pay the price for this cruel, unlawful, and barbaric tactic.

33

The Empty Spaces in Gaza

August 6, 2014

H ow many times have you heard on television or
read in the media that the Gaza Strip is "the most
densely populated area in the world"? Repeating
this statement, however, does not make it true. There are
dense parts of Gaza, especially Gaza City, Beit Hanoun,
and Khan Younis, but there are far less dense areas in Gaza
between these cities. Just look at this population density
map.[1] Or look at Google Earth.

The fact that these sparsely populated areas exist in the
Gaza Strip raise several important moral questions: First,
why don't the media show the relatively open areas of the
Gaza Strip? Why do they only show the densely populated
cities? There are several possible reasons. There is no fighting
going on in the sparsely populated areas, so showing them
would be boring. But that's precisely the point—to show areas from which Hamas could be firing rockets and building
tunnels but has chosen not to. Or perhaps the reason the
media doesn't show these areas is that Hamas won't let them.
That too would be a story worth reporting.

1 See http://news.bbc.co.uk/2/shared/spl/hi/middle_east/03/
v3_israel_palestinians/maps/html/population_settlements.stm.

Second, why doesn't Hamas use sparsely populated areas from which to launch its rockets and build its tunnels? Were it to do so, Palestinian civilian casualties would decrease dramatically, but the casualty rate among Hamas terrorists would increase dramatically.

That is precisely why Hamas selects the most densely populated areas from which to fire and dig. The difference between Israel and Hamas is that Israel uses its soldiers to protect its civilians, whereas Hamas uses its civilians to protect its terrorists. That is why most Israeli casualties have been soldiers and most of Hamas's casualties have been civilians. The other reason is that Israel builds shelters for its civilians, whereas Hamas builds shelters only for its terrorists, intending that most of the casualties be among its civilian shields.

The law is clear: using civilians as human shields—which the Hamas battle manual mandates—is an absolute war crime. There are no exceptions or matters of degree, especially when there are alternatives. On the other hand, shooting at legitimate military targets, such as rockets and terror tunnels, is permitted, unless the number of anticipated civilian casualties is disproportionate to the military importance of the target. This is a matter of degree and judgment, often difficult to calculate in the fog of war. The law is also clear that when a criminal takes a hostage and uses that hostage as a shield from behind whom to fire at civilians or police, and if the police fire back and kill the hostage, it is the criminal and not the policeman who is guilty of murder. So too with Hamas: when it uses human shields and the Israeli army fires back and kills some of the shields, it is Hamas who is responsible for their deaths.

The third moral question is why does the United Nations try to shelter Palestinian civilians right in the middle of the areas from which Hamas is firing? Hamas has decided not to use the less densely populated areas for rocket firing and tunnel digging. For that reason, the United Nations should use these sparsely populated areas as places of refuge. Since the Gaza Strip is relatively small, it would not be difficult to move civilians to these safer areas. They should declare these areas battle free and build temporary shelters—tents if necessary—as places of asylum for the residents of the crowded cities. It should prevent any Hamas fighters, any rockets, and any tunnel builders from entering into these sanctuaries. In that way, Hamas would be denied the use of human shields and Israel would have no reason to fire its rockets anywhere near these United Nations sanctuaries. The net result would be a considerable saving of lives.

But instead the UN is playing right into the hands of Hamas by sheltering civilians right next to Hamas fighters, Hamas weapons, and Hamas tunnels. Then the United Nations and the international community accuses Israel of doing precisely what Hamas intended Israel to do: namely fire at its terrorists and kill United Nations–protected civilians in the process. It's a cynical game being played by Hamas, but it wouldn't succeed without the complicity of UN agencies.

The only way to assure that Hamas's strategy of using human shields to maximize civilian casualties is not repeated over and over again is for the international community, and especially the United Nations, not to encourage and facilitate it, as it currently does. International law must be enforced against Hamas for its double war crime: using civilian human shields to fire at civilian Israeli targets. If this tactic were to be brought to a halt, then Israel would have no need to respond in self-defense. Applying the laws of war to Israel alone will do no good, because any country faced with rockets and tunnels targeting its civilians will fight back. When the fighters and tunnel builders hide behind human shields, there will inevitably be civilian casualties—unintended by Israel, intended by Hamas—regardless of how careful the defenders are. Israel has tried its hardest to minimize civilian casualties. Hamas has tried its hardest to maximize civilian casualties. Now the United Nations and the international community must try their hardest to become part of the solution rather than part of the problem.

34

Hamas Exaggerates
Civilian Deaths

August 8, 2014

I T'S A MYSTERY why so many in the media accept as gospel Hamas-supplied figures on the number of civilians killed in the recent war.

Hamas claims that of the more than 1800 Palestinians killed, close to 90 percent were civilians. Israel, on the other hand, says that close to half of them were combatants.

The objective facts support a number much closer to Israel's than to Hamas's.

Even human rights groups antagonistic to Israel acknowledge, according to a New York Times report,[1] that Hamas probably counts among the "civilians killed by Israel" the following groups: Palestinians killed by Hamas as collaborators; Palestinians killed through domestic violence; Palestinians killed by errant Hamas rockets or mortars; and Palestinians who died naturally during the conflict.

I wonder if Hamas also included the reported 162 children who died while performing child slave labor in

---

1 Jodi Rudoren, "Civilian or Not? New Fight in Tallying the Dead from Gaza Conflict," the *New York Times*, 5 August 2014.

building their terror tunnels. Hamas also defines combatants to include only armed fighters who were killed while fighting Israelis. They exclude Hamas supporters who build tunnels, who allow their homes to be used to store and fire rockets, Hamas policemen, members of the Hamas political wing, and others who work hand in hand with the armed terrorists.

Several years ago I came up with a concept which I call the "continuum of civilianality"—an inelegant phrase that is intended to convey the reality that who is a civilian and who is a combatant is often a matter of degree.

Clearly every child below the age in which he or she is capable of assisting Hamas is a civilian. Clearly every Hamas fighter who fires rockets, bears arms, or operates in the tunnels is a combatant. Between these extremes lies a wide range of people, some of whom are closer to the civilian end, many of whom are closer to the combatant end.

The law of war has not established a clear line between combatants and civilians, especially in the context of urban warfare where people carry guns at night and bake bread during the day, or fire rockets during the day and go back home to sleep with their families at night. (Interestingly, the Israeli Supreme Court has tried to devise a functional definition of combatants in the murky context of urban guerilla warfare.)

Data published by the *New York Times*[2] strongly suggests that a very large number—perhaps a majority—of those killed are closer to the combatant end of the continuum than to the civilian end. First of all, the vast majority of those killed have been male rather than female. In an Islamic society, males are far more likely to be combatants than females. Second, most of those killed who are within the age range of fifteen to forty are likely to be combatants. The vast

2 Ibid.

majority of these are male as well. The number of people over sixty who have been killed is infinitesimal. The number of children below the age of fifteen is also relatively small, although their pictures have been shown more frequently than others.

In other words, the genders and ages of those killed are not representative of the general population of Gaza. It is far more representative of the genders and ages of combatants. These data strongly suggest that a very large percentage of Palestinians killed are on the combatant side of the continuum.

They also prove, as if any proof were necessary to unbiased eyes, that Israel did not target civilians randomly. If it had, the dead would be representative of the Gaza population in general, rather than of the subgroups most closely identified with combatants.

The media should immediately stop using Hamas-approved statistics, which in the past have proved to be extremely unreliable. Instead, they should try to document, independently, the nature of each person killed and describe their age, gender, occupation, affiliation with Hamas, and other objective factors relevant to their status as a combatant, noncombatant, or someone in the middle.

It is lazy and dangerous for the media to rely on Hamas-approved propaganda figures. In fact, when the infamous *Goldstone Report* falsely stated that the vast majority of people killed in Operation Cast Lead were civilians and not Hamas fighters, many in Gaza complained to Hamas. They accused Hamas of cowardice for allowing so many civilians to be killed while protecting their own fighters. As a result of these complaints, Hamas was forced to tell the truth, namely that many more of those killed were actually Hamas fighters or armed policemen.

It is likely that Hamas will make a similar correction

with regard to this conflict. But that correction will not be covered by the media, as the prior correction was not.

The headline "Most of those killed by Israel were children, women, and the elderly" will continue to be the conventional wisdom, despite its factual falsity.

Unless it is corrected, Hamas will continue with its dead baby strategy and more people on both sides will die.

AUTHOR'S NOTE

On September 2, 2014, an Israeli military intelligence spokesperson issued the following figures on Palestinian deaths:

Hamas operatives	341
Members of Islamic Jihad	182
Other Combatants	93
Total combatants to date	616
Civilians to date	706
Unknown, not yet categorized as combatants or civilians	805

The spokesperson also said 857 Hamas rockets landed inside Gaza, killing and wounding an undetermined number of people. The official said some of the Hamas rockets "were fired intentionally at the local Palestinian population." This was based on what was seen "in the system." Additional evidence was also presented of the deliberate use of schools as locations from which to fire rockets:

> The intelligence official presented more evidence to bolster Israel's assertions that Hamas waged its campaign largely by hiding behind its own civilians. An aerial photograph appeared to show a rocket firing site in the yard of a school in Shejaiya. In before and after pictures, a

fabric canopy believed to be hiding the rockets appeared intact, then ripped. Another previously unpublished photograph showed a schoolyard in Beit Lahiya that was empty by day. By night, it was dotted with what looked like several rockets laid out on the ground and boxes that the official said contained more rockets.[3]

This evidence supplemented other videos and photographs showing rockets being fired from near United Nations facilities, schools, hospitals, and other civilian areas, as well as tunnel entrances in prayer rooms of mosques.

Expert testimony presented before a Knesset Committee confirms the accuracy of the Israeli assessment.[4] On September 4, 2014, the *Jerusalem Post* reported that:

Israel's ratio of civilian to military casualties in Operation Protective Edge was only one-fourth of the average in warfare around the world, former commander of British forces in Afghanistan Col. (res.) Richard Kemp told the Knesset Foreign Affairs and Defense Committee Wednesday.

Kemp pointed out that, during the operation, there was approximately one civilian casualty for every terrorist killed by the IDF, whereas the average in the world is four civilians for every combatant, and that, when taking into

---

3 Isabel Kershner, "Israel Says Hamas is Hurt Significantly," the *New York Times*, 2 September 2014.

4 For somewhat different numbers, see: "Occupied Palestinian Territory: Gaza Emergency Situation Report (as of 4 September 2014, 0800 hrs)," United Nations Office of Coordination of Humanitarian Affairs, 4 September 2014.

consideration Hamas's use of human shields, this shows how careful the IDF is.

"No army in the world acts with as much discretion and great care as the IDF in order to minimize damage. The US and the UK are careful, but not as much as Israel," he told the committee.[5]

5 Lahav Harkov, "Former British Commander in Afghanistan: No Army Acts with as Much Discretion as IDF Does," *The Jerusalem Post*, 4 September 2014.

35

Supporting Hamas
Is Anti-Semitic

August 14, 2014

CRITICIZING SPECIFIC ISRAELI POLICIES is certainly not anti-Semitic. Indeed many Israelis are critical of some of their nation's policies. But support for Hamas *is* anti-Semitic, because Hamas's policies and actions are based, at their core, on Jew hatred.

Yet many prominent individuals, some out of ignorance, many more with full knowledge of what they are doing, are overtly supporting Hamas. Some have even praised it. Others, like Italy's most famous philosopher, Gianni Vattimo, are trying to raise money and provide material support to this anti-Semitic terrorist organization. Still others refuse to condemn it, while condemning Israel in the strongest terms.

Here is some of what the Hamas Charter, which remains its governing principles, says about Jews:

> The enemies have been scheming for a long time. [Their] wealth [permitted them to] take over control of the world media such as news agencies, the press, publication houses, broadcasting, and the like. [They also used this] wealth to stir revolutions in various parts of the globe...

They stood behind the French and the Communist Revolutions… They also used the money to establish clandestine organizations which are spreading around the world, in order to destroy societies and carry out Zionist interests.

Such organizations are: the Freemasons, Rotary Clubs, Lions Clubs, B'nai B'rith, and the like. All of them are destructive spying organizations… [T]hey stood behind World War I, so as to wipe out the Islamic Caliphate… They obtained the Balfour Declaration and established the League of Nations in order to rule the world by means of that organization. They also stood behind World War ii… They inspired the establishment of the United Nations and the Security Council to replace the League of Nations, in order to rule the world by their intermediary. There was no war that broke out anywhere without their fingerprints on it…

Most of these references to "the enemies" precede the establishment of Israel. The charter plainly means "the Jews," and it invokes the usual tropes of anti-Semitism and Jew hatred. Indeed, it expressly calls for the murder of Jews, citing Islamic sources for its genocidal goal:

Hamas has been looking forward to implement Allah's promise whatever time it might take. The prophet, prayer and peace be upon him, said: The time will not come until Muslims will fight the Jews; until the Jews hide behind rocks and trees, which will cry: O Muslim! There is a Jew hiding behind me, come on and kill him!

This should not be surprising news. Hamas is a wholly owned subsidiary of the Muslim Brotherhood, which is an outgrowth of the German Nazi Party. The brotherhood was founded in 1928 by Hassan al-Banna, a close ally of Adolph Hitler. It worked hand in hand with Hitler during World War II, establishing the Muslim Waffen-ss Handschar division, which committed war crimes against Jewish communities. It then helped to rescue Nazi war criminals following the defeat of Nazism and the disclosure of the Holocaust.

Nor is the charter and the origin of Hamas merely past history. Current Hamas leaders frequently invoke the "blood libel," accusing "the Jews" of killing Christian children and using their blood for the baking of matzo. They regard Jewish places of worship and Jewish schools, anywhere in the world, as appropriate targets for their terrorist attacks.

Some of those who support Hamas, such as Jimmy Carter and Mary Robinson, claim that they support its political goals, but not its anti-Semitic policies. (They must recognize "its legitimacy as a political actor.") Others, such as the Turkish Foreign Minister and the leaders of Qatar, support its military goals. (They support the Palestinian resistance movement Hamas "because it embraces the Palestinian cause and struggles for its people.")

An American literature professor, Judith Butler, has gone so far as to call Hamas a social movement that is "progressive," "on the left," and "part of a global left." But what other progressive and left groups murder gays, oppress women and prevent non-Muslims from practicing their religions? As a Jewish woman, Butler would not fare well in a Hamas environment. Nevertheless, she supports this murderous anti-Semitic group because of its "progressive" social policies.

These specious rationales hold no water, since Hamas's anti-Jewish policies are central to its political and military actions. Some supporters of Hitler made the same argument, claiming that the Nazi Party and its leaders espoused good economic, educational, and political policies. No reasonable person today accepts that excuse, and no reasonable person should accept the excuses offered by supporters of Hamas who claim to be able to slice the bologna so thin.

The same is true for those who argue that Hamas is preferable to ISIS or other jihadist groups that might replace it. A similar argument was made by fascists who claimed that their parties were preferable to the Communists. The reality is that Hamas is an anti-Semitic organization, based on a Jew-hating philosophy, with the goal of destroying the nation-state of the Jewish people and killing its Jewish inhabitants. It is evil personified. There is no excuse or justification for supporting Hamas, and anyone who does is supporting anti-Semitism.

Some Hamas supporters—such as those who chant "Hamas, Hamas, Jews to the gas"—proudly acknowledge this reality. Others, such as Cornell West, who according to the American Spectator "headlined a high-profile pro-Hamas demonstration,"[1] deny it. But all are complicit, even if they are themselves Jewish or have Jewish friends.

Supporting an organization that at its core is anti-Jewish and whose charter calls for the killing of all Jews *is* anti-Semitic in effect if not in intent. And those politicians, academics, entertainers, and others who support Hamas—and there are many—must be called out and condemned, as Roger Waters of rock band Pink Floyd has been.

So must those, like Navi Pillay, the head of the United Nations Human Rights Council, who see a moral equivalence between this anti-Semitic terrorist group and the democratic nation-state of the Jewish people. She demanded that Israel share its Iron Dome system with Hamas, without condemning Hamas for using Palestinian civilians as its own Iron Dome.

1 Jed Babbin, "Hamas's Cheerleaders," *The American Spectator*, 4 August 2014.

Among the worst offenders is Bishop Desmond Tutu, who has a long history of anti-Semitism. He, like Carter, has urged recognition of Hamas, whose leaders he compares to Nelson Mandela. Among Tutu's alleged Mandelas with whom he has collaborated is Ahmad Abu Halabiya, who has said the following:

"Have no mercy on the Jews, no matter where they are, in any country. Fight them, wherever you are. Wherever you meet them, kill them... and those Americans who are like them, and those who stand by them."[2]

I'm quite certain the real Nelson Mandela never made any comparable statement. Yet Bishop Tutu, who refused to sit on the same stage as Tony Blair, has worked hand in hand with murderous Hamas leaders such as Halabiya.

It may be necessary to negotiate—directly or through intermediaries—with Hamas, just as one negotiates with kidnappers, hostage takers, or extortionists. But to recognize their legitimacy as Jimmy Carter and Bishop Tutu would do is to recognize the legitimacy of anti-Semitism.

Carter, Tutu, and other Hamas cheerleaders may be willing to do that, but no reasonable person who hates bigotry should legitimate Hamas's anti-Semitism or its express goal of destroying Israel and killing its Jewish inhabitants.

Nor should any reasonable person accept the anti-Semitism inherent in what has come to be called "Holocaust inversion"—namely "calling the Israelis Nazis and likening Gaza to the Warsaw Ghetto."[3] Turkey's president has indulged in this form of bigotry, as have several Columbia University faculty members, such as Professor Hamid Dabashi. Here is what Dabashi said:

2 See https://www.youtube.com/watch?v=0ILBF7iBw_A.
3 See Martin Kramer, "Gaza = Auschwitz", *Mosaic*, 26 August 2014.

After Gaza, not a single living Israeli can utter the word "Auschwitz" without it sounding like "Gaza." Auschwitz as a historical fact is now archival. Auschwitz as a metaphor is now Palestinian. From now on, every time any Israeli, *every time any Jew*, anywhere in the world, utters the word "Auschwitz," or the word "Holocaust," the world will hear "Gaza." (emphasis added.)

This perverse inversion was invented by Soviet propagandists when Stalin turned against Israel and Jewish "cosmopolitans." It has now become a staple of radical Islam and the hard left. It has also become another variation on Holocaust denial and minimization. As Howard Jacobson, the winner of the prestigious Man Booker Prize, aptly put it:

Berating Jews with their own history, disinheriting them of pity, as though pity is negotiable or has a sell-by date, is the latest species of Holocaust denial... The modern sophisticated denier accepts the event in all its terrible enormity, only to accuse the Jews of trying to profit from it, either in the form of moral blackmail or downright territorial theft. According to this thinking, the Jews have betrayed the Holocaust and become unworthy of it, the true heirs to their suffering being the Palestinians.

Yet another species of anti-Semitism—this one dating from time immemorial—is to punish or threaten one group of Jews for the alleged sins of another group of Jews. This phenomenon occurred recently in South Africa, where a leader of the Congress of South African Trades Unions called for "an eye for an eye against Zionist aggression." He went on to insist that "if a woman or child is killed in Gaza," then South African Jews, especially members of the Jewish Board of Deputies, must suffer revenge, based on the principle of eye for eye, life for life.

These then are the newest forms of anti-Semitic bigotry: support for organizations, such as Hamas, that overtly call for the murder of Jews and the destruction of Israel; comparing Israel's efforts to protect its citizens against rocket attacks and tunnel-terrorism to the Nazi's efforts, largely successful, to exterminate every Jew in the world; and demanding revenge against Jews for the military actions of Israel. All are equally shameful and worthy of rebuke.

36

Did Israel Have the Right to Destroy Hamas Terror Tunnels?

August 19, 2014

THE KEY QUESTION—both legally and morally—in evaluating Israel's recent military actions is whether the Israeli government was justified in ordering ground troops into Gaza to destroy the Hamas tunnels. This question is important because most of the deaths—among Palestinian civilians, Hamas terrorists, and Israeli soldiers—came about after Israeli ground troops attacked the tunnels.

These tunnels went deep underground from Gaza to Israel and were designed to allow Hamas death squads to cross into Israel and to kill and kidnap Israeli citizens. No reasonable person can dispute that these terrorist tunnels were legitimate military targets.

Nor could there be any dispute about their importance as military targets, since Hamas was planning to use them to murder and kidnap hundreds if not thousands of Israeli civilians and soldiers. And Israel had no way to discover from the air the exit points from these tunnels on the Israel side of the border, since they were hidden from view and known only to Hamas. The only way to disable them was through boots on the ground.

If Israel had the right to try to destroy the tunnels, then the resulting deaths of Palestinians must be deemed proportional to the military value of Israel's actions, since it is unlikely that the tunnels could have been destroyed without considerable loss of life, because their entrances had been deliberately placed by Hamas in densely populated areas.

The law is clear that military targets may be attacked, even if civilian casualties are anticipated, so long as the importance of the military target is proportional to the anticipated civilian casualties and that reasonable efforts are made, consistent with military needs, to minimize civilian casualties.

This sensible rule of proportionality was devised in the context of ordinary military encounters, in which the enemy is not using their own civilians as human shields. If the enemy is deliberately using civilians as human shields, the rules of proportionality should allow for more anticipated civilian casualties, especially if the target is of great military significance, as these terror tunnels were.

The reason that civilian casualties, as well as military casualties among both Hamas terrorists and Israeli soldiers, could be anticipated, is because the entrance to these terror tunnels were deliberately placed by Hamas in densely populated civilian areas, including mosques, schools, and private homes. These tunnels could not be destroyed from the air without causing a far greater number of civilian casualties than those resulting from a ground attack.

Moreover, the only way to ensure their destruction was for ground troops to go from tunnel to tunnel and to blow them up one by one. This inevitably risked civilian casualties. Had Hamas built the entrance to the tunnels in the many open areas of the Gaza Strip, away from the most densely populated urban centers, the number of civilian casualties would have been considerably reduced.

Hamas thus made a calculated decision to put the Israeli government to a difficult choice: either allow the tunnels to remain, thus risking the lives of thousands of Israeli civilians; or send ground troops into densely populated areas to destroy the tunnels, thus risking the lives of Palestinian civilians and Israeli soldiers. Every democracy in the world would choose the latter option if faced with this tragic and cruel choice. That is why the laws of war authorized Israel to do what it had to do to destroy the tunnels.

To be sure, the law of proportionality also required Israel to take reasonable steps, consistent with its military needs, to minimize Palestinian civilian casualties, even when attacking legitimate military targets. The key word here is "reasonable," and Israel has gone well beyond what other countries have done in analogous situations. They issued warnings by leaflet, phone, and other means—warnings that Hamas countermanded in its efforts to keep civilians in harm's way and continue to have them serve as human shields to protect their terror tunnels.

Israel did not issue warnings when it needed to act quickly to save its own soldiers from ambushes and other serious risks. Israel thus tried to minimize Palestinian civilian casualties, while Hamas tried to increase both Palestinian and Israeli civilian casualties.

The Israeli government is conducting several investigations as to whether any of its soldiers violated its carefully designed rules of engagement that were drafted by lawyers familiar with international law. If they did not, then there is no valid legal or moral case against Israel. If they did and are prosecuted by Israeli authorities—either military or civilian—then the rules of the International Criminal Court would preclude it from bringing charges against any Israelis.

The right of Israel to target these terrorist tunnels is thus central to any analysis of the legal consequences of civilian deaths in Gaza. Yet a recent report by a group of self-described legal experts that accused Israel of war crimes did not even mention the tunnels.

This report, deceptively entitled "Joint Declaration by International Law Experts on Israel's Gaza Offensive,"[1] also deliberately ignored the facts that Hamas combatants do not wear uniforms, repeatedly fired rockets and mortars from densely populated civilian areas, and stored weapons and ammunition in and around mosques, schools, and designated refugee centers—all in violation of the laws of war.

Legally, the report misrepresents a crucial dimension of International Law by claiming that Israel violated the principle of distinction by targeting civilian buildings, without mentioning that a civilian structure becomes a legitimate military target when it is used for military purposes.

More serious is the accusation that Israel committed the war crime of collective punishment by deliberately attacking the civilian population. Again, this is a blatant mischaracterization, both of Israel's actions which were preventive rather than punitive in nature, and a willful misappropriation of a term defined in the context of mass executions during World War II.

Hamas knows that in the modern media environment it profits from the deaths of Palestinian civilians, so much so that it repeatedly refused cease-fire offers proposed both by Israel and international mediators. The vast majority of Palestinian deaths came after Hamas refused to accept these cease-fires.

The title of the report is doubly deceptive because very few of its signatories are recognized experts in international law. Those who are—such as Richard Falk, John Dugard,

---

1 Richard Falk, "Joint Declaration by International Law Experts on Israel's Gaza Offensive," *Global Justice in the 21st Century* (blog), 28 July 2014.

and Peter Weiss—have notorious reputations as anti-Zionist zealots. The very fact that they labeled Israeli defensive actions as offensive demonstrates their bias.

No self-respecting lawyer would ever file a brief making the kind of unsubstantiated factual and legal claims made by this report. Were a lawyer to file a brief that did not mention the most salient facts that undercut its conclusion—here the tunnels and use of human shields—that lawyer would be disciplined, perhaps even disbarred. This report is a disgrace to the legal profession and to the academic institutions—such as Boston University, Georgetown, and UCLA—whose names are highlighted for identification purposes. Its biased authors should be called to account for this unprofessional and unethical document, and no credibility should be accorded it by fair-minded people concerned for the truth.

Nor should people of good will pay any attention to Bishop Desmond Tutu's most recent screed, accusing Israel of conducting a "disproportionally brutal" military attack and "indiscriminate killing" in Gaza. Tutu also deliberately fails to mention the terrorist terror tunnels, as if by ignoring them, they would stop posing a lethal threat to thousands of Israeli citizens.

Those who condemn Israel's recent military actions have an obligation to answer the following questions: Did Israel have the right to try to prevent those terror tunnels from being used to murder and kidnap its citizens? If so, how could Israel have accomplished that with substantially fewer casualties?

37

ISIS is to America
as Hamas is to Israel

August 21, 2014

P RESIDENT BARACK OBAMA has rightfully condemned the ISIS beheading of American James Foley
in the strongest terms. This is what he said:

> There has to be a common effort to extract this cancer
> so it does not spread. There has to be a clear rejection
> of these kind of nihilistic ideologies. One thing we can
> all agree on is a group like (ISIS) has no place in the 21st
> century. Friends and allies around the world, we share a
> common security, a set of values opposite of what we saw
> yesterday. We will continue to confront this hateful ter-
> rorism and replace it with a sense of hope and stability.[1]

At the same time that President Obama has called for
an all-out war against the "cancer" of ISIS, he has regarded

1 Barack Obama, "Statement by the President," (speech, Martha's Vineyard,
MA, August 20, 2014). Since that time another American, Steven Sotloff,
was also beheaded by ISIS. He was an American Jew, who also held Israeli
citizenship.

Hamas as having an easily curable disease, urging Israel to accept that terrorist group, whose charter calls for Israel's destruction, as part of a Palestinian unity government. I cannot imagine him urging Iraq, or any other Arab country, to accept ISIS as part of a unity government.

Former President Jimmy Carter and Bishop Desmond Tutu have gone even further, urging the international community to recognize the legitimacy of Hamas as a political party and to grant it diplomatic recognition. It is hard to imagine them demanding that the same legitimate status be accorded ISIS.

Why then the double standard regarding ISIS and Hamas? Is it because ISIS is less brutal and violent than Hamas? It's hard to make that case. Hamas has probably killed at least as many civilians—through its suicide bombs, its murder of Palestinian Authority members, its rocket attacks and its terror tunnels—than ISIS has done. If not for Israel's Iron Dome and the Israeli Defense Forces, Hamas would have killed even more innocent civilians. Indeed its charter calls for the killing of all Jews anywhere in the world, regardless of where they live or which "rock" they are hiding behind. If Hamas had its way, it would kill at least as many people as ISIS would.

Is it the *manner* by which ISIS kills? Beheading is of course a visibly grotesque means of killing, but dead is dead and murder is murder. And it matters little to the victim's family whether the death was caused by beheading, by hanging, or by a bullet in the back of a head. Indeed most of ISIS's victims have been shot rather than beheaded, while Hamas terrorists have slaughtered innocent babies in their beds, teenagers on the way home from school, women shopping, Jews praying, and students eating pizza.

Is it because ISIS murdered an American? Hamas has murdered numerous Americans and citizens of other countries. They too are indiscriminate in who they kill.

Is it because ISIS has specifically threatened to bring its terrorism to American shores, while Hamas focuses its terrorism in Israel? The Hamas Charter does not limit its murderous intentions to one country. Like ISIS it calls for a worldwide caliphate, brought about by violent jihad.

Everything we rightly fear and despise from ISIS we should fear and despise from Hamas. Just as we would never grant legitimacy to ISIS, we should not grant legitimacy to Hamas—at the very least until it rescinds its charter and renounces violence. Unfortunately that is about as likely as America rescinding its constitution. Violence, anti-Semitism, and anti-Americanism are the sine qua non of Hamas's mission.

Just as ISIS must be defeated militarily and destroyed as a terrorist army, so too must Hamas be responded to militarily and its rockets and tunnels destroyed.

It is widely, and in my view mistakenly, argued by many academics and diplomats that there can never be a military solution to terrorism in general or to the demands of Hamas in particular. This conventional wisdom ignores the lessons of history. Chamberlain thought there could be a diplomatic solution to Hitler's demands. Churchill disagreed. History proved Churchill correct. Nazi Fascists and Japanese militarists had to be defeated militarily before a diplomatic resolution could be achieved.

So too with ISIS and Hamas. They must first be defeated militarily, and only then might they consider accepting reasonable diplomatic and political compromises. Another similarity between ISIS and Hamas is that if these terrorist groups were to lay down their arms, there might be peace, whereas if their enemies were to lay down *their* arms, there would be genocide.

A wonderful cartoon illustrates this: at one end of the

table is Hamas demanding "Death to all Jews." At the other end is Israel's Prime Minister Netanyahu. In the middle sits the mediator, who turns to Netanyahu and asks: "Could you at least meet him halfway?"

No democratic nation can accept its own destruction. We cannot compromise—come halfway—with terrorists who demand the deaths of all who stand in the way of their demand for a Sunni caliphate, whether these terrorists call themselves ISIS or Hamas. Both are, in the words of President Obama, "cancers" that must be extracted before they spread. Both are equally malignant. Both must be defeated on the battlefield, in the court of public opinion, and in the courts of law. There can be no compromise with bigotry, terrorism, or the demand for a caliphate. Before Hamas or ISIS can be considered legitimate political partners, they must give up their violent quest for a worldwide Islamic caliphate.

AUTHOR'S NOTE

On 5 September, 2004, President Barak Obama announced that a coalition of American allies would seek to "dismantle," "degrade," and "destroy" ISIS:

> You initially push them back, you systematically degrade their capabilities, you narrow their scope of action, you slowly shrink the space, the territory that they control, you take out their leadership, and, over time, they are not able to conduct the same kinds of terrorist attacks that they once could.[2]

This sounds quite similar to the military approach taken by Israel against Hamas, which poses a far greater threat

2 Helen Cooper, "Obama Enlists 9 Allies to Help in the Battle Against ISIS," the *New York Times*, 5 September 2014.

to neighboring Israel than ISIS poses to faraway America. Indeed on 8 September 2014, Reuters reported that the United States has been seeking intelligence support from Israel to assist in its campaign against ISIS.[3] Yet Israel is accused by many of war crimes for taking the same actions as the United States and its allies.

3 Dan Williams, "Israel Provides anti-Islamic State Coalition with Intelligence, Says Western Diplomat," *Haaretz*, 8 September 2014, quoting Reuters.

38

No One Should Be Surprised at ISIS's Brutality because the World Rewards Terrorism

September 4, 2014

THE INTERNATIONAL COMMUNITY seems to have been caught off guard by the brutality of ISIS. The beheading of two Americans, the murder of many Christians and Muslims, and the widespread support for these brutal killers has taken the world by surprise. But we should have anticipated this, because for the last half century, the international community has rewarded precisely the kind of behavior by ISIS we now condemn. In brief, terrorism has proved to be a successful tactic. It works. That's why ISIS engages in it. That's why al-Qaeda engages in it. That's why Boko Haram engages in it. That's why the Taliban engages in it. And that's why Hamas engages in it.

Compare the visibility and success of groups that employ terrorism as the main tactic for responding to their grievances, with comparably aggrieved groups that reject terrorism. Hamas is more popular than ever among Palestinians following their kidnapping and murder of three Israeli schoolchildren, their brutal slaughter of the Fogel family, and their deployment of rockets and tunnels against civilians from civilian areas. The same is true of Hezbollah.

Now comes ISIS which is quickly becoming the terrorist group of choice for disaffected radicals, because their brutality is now in the headlines.

Contrast these successes with the failure of the Tibetan people to achieve much attention or progress in their quest to end an occupation even longer than the one Israel is accused of maintaining. The world demands statehood for the Palestinians, while allowing the Kurds to remain stateless despite treaty obligations and other promises. Why? Is it because the Tibetans and Kurds have rarely engaged in terrorism, whereas the Palestinians have specialized in it since the establishment of the Palestine Liberation Organization in the early 1960s—and even before that?

Success begets emulation, and the success of terrorist organizations is spreading quickly. No one should be surprised.

ISIS has already achieved success as a result of their brutal terrorist acts. Millions of dollars have been paid to them as ransom for hostages. They have used this money to recruit more members. Now other Muslim terrorist groups want to join forces with them, because they have shown that within the world of brutal terrorism, they stand out for their unmitigated and televised brutality.

Consider the following hypothetical situation. A new group with a serious grievance hires an amoral consulting firm to advise them on the most effective tactic for achieving their goals. Such a consulting group might well recommend that they emulate Hamas, ISIS, al-Qaeda and other terrorist groups, rather than the Tibetans or Kurds. This advice would of course be immoral but it would be truthful as a matter of simple cost-benefit analysis.

In the end, the only way to defeat terrorism is to reverse the cost-benefit calculus. This would require an international agreement whereby every country in the world would pledge to refuse to give in to terrorists, to pay ransom to terrorists, to legitimate terrorist organizations or to treat them as morally and politically equivalent to the democracies they are fighting. It would also require that no country release captured terrorists from custody and that they place them on trial or extradite them to a country that will.

We are doing exactly the opposite today. World leaders, such as Jimmy Carter and Desmond Tutu, demand that we treat Hamas, which is indistinguishable in its overall brutality from isis, as a legitimate political organization. The United Nations General Assembly grants statehood to a group that began as a terrorist organization and continues to honor terrorists who murdered children. The Nobel Peace Prize Committee honors Yasser Arafat, the godfather of terrorism, who persisted in this tactic until the day he died. European countries pay ransom to terrorists. And many European nations—Italy, Germany, Great Britain, and others—have freed terrorists, including mass murderers, who have returned to lives of terror. Even Israel has engaged in prisoner exchanges with terrorist groups.

It is one thing to negotiate—directly or indirectly—with terrorists who hold innocent people as hostages. Such negotiation may be a necessary evil. Democratic nations are sometimes forced to negotiate with the Mafia, the Ku Klux Klan, and other criminal gangs. But we should never honor or legitimate them, as we have done with Palestinian terrorists. Nor should the world condemn and place on trial democracies that fight against terrorist organizations that use their own civilians as human shields. The current misguided approach is a prescription for emulation and repetition of terrorism as the tactic of choice.

So let's not be surprised when a group like isis learns the tragic lesson of history and emulates success and visibility rather than failure and invisibility. ISIS is doing exactly what the amoral consulting firm would advise it to do. So we shouldn't be surprised. Instead we should reverse course and develop responses to terrorism that never allow this tactic to succeed. Terrorists must never be allowed to win, as they are, unfortunately, doing today.

39

Ten Reasons Why BDS Is Immoral and Hinders Peace

February 12, 2014

T HE BDS MOVEMENT, which will only increase following the 2014 war in Gaza, is highly immoral, threatens the peace process, and discourages the Palestinians from agreeing to any reasonable peace offer. Here are ten compelling reasons why the BDS movement is immoral and incompatible with current efforts to arrive at a compromise peace.

1. The BDS movement immorally imposes the entire blame for the continuing Israeli occupation and settlement policy on the Israelis.

It refuses to acknowledge the historical reality that on at least three occasions, Israel offered to end the occupation and on all three occasions, the Palestinian leadership, supported by its people, refused to accept these offers. In 1967, I played a small role in drafting UN Security Council Resolution 242 that set out the formula for ending the occupation in exchange for recognition of Israel's right to exist in peace. Israel accepted that resolution, while the Palestinians, along with all the Arab nations, gathered in Khartoum and issued their three famous noes: no peace, no negotiation, no recognition. There were no efforts to boycott, sanction, or divest from these Arabs naysayers. In 2000 and 2001, Israel's liberal prime minister Ehud Barak, along with American president Bill Clinton, offered the Palestinians statehood and the end of the occupation. Yasser Arafat rejected this offer—a rejection that many Arab leaders considered a crime against the Palestinian people. In 2007, Israel's prime minister Ehud Olmert offered the Palestinians an even better deal, an offer to which they failed to respond. There were no BDS threats against those who rejected Israel's peace offers. Hopefully, there will be ongoing peace negotiations in which both parties make offers. Under the circumstances, it is immoral to impose blame only on Israel and to direct a BDS movement only against the nation-state of the Jewish people, which has thrice offered to end the occupation in exchange for peace.

2. The current BDS movement, especially in Europe and on some American university campuses, emboldens the Palestinians to reject compromise solutions to the conflict.

Some within the Palestinian leadership have told me that the longer they hold out against making peace, the more powerful will be the BDS movement against Israel. Why not wait until BDS strengthens their bargaining position so that they won't have to compromise by giving up the right of return, by agreeing to a demilitarized state, and by making other concessions that are necessary to peace but difficult for some Palestinians to accept? The BDS movement is making a peaceful resolution harder.

3. The BDS movement is immoral because its leaders will never be satisfied with the kind of two-state solution that is acceptable to Israel.

Many of its leaders do not believe in the concept of Israel as the nation-state of the Jewish people. (The major leader of the BDS movement, Omar Barghouti, has repeatedly expressed his opposition to Israel's right to exist as the nation-state of the Jewish people even within the 1967 borders.) At bottom, therefore, the leadership of the BDS movement is opposed not only to Israel's occupation and settlement policy but to its very existence.

4. The BDS movement is immoral because it violates the core principle of human rights: namely, "the worst first."

Israel is among the freest and most democratic nations in the world. It is certainly the freest and most democratic nation in the Middle East. Its Arab citizens enjoy more rights than Arabs anywhere else in the world. They serve in the Knesset, in the judiciary, in the foreign service, in the academy, and in business. They are free to criticize Israel and to support its enemies. Israeli universities are hotbeds of anti-Israel rhetoric, advocacy, and even teaching. Israel has a superb record on women's rights, gay rights, environmental rights, and other rights that barely exist in most parts of the world. Moreover, Israel's record of avoiding civilian casualties, while fighting enemies who hide their soldiers among civilians, is unparalleled in the world today. The situation on the West Bank is obviously different because of the occupation, but even the Arabs of Ramallah, Bethlehem, and Tulkarm have more human and political rights than the vast majority of Arabs in the world today. Moreover, anyone—Jew, Muslim, or Christian—dissatisfied with Israeli actions can express that dissatisfaction in the courts, and in the media, both at home and abroad. That freedom does not exist in any Arab country, or in many non-Arab countries. Yet Israel is the only country in the world today being threatened with BDS. When a sanction is directed only against a state with one of the best records of human rights, and that nation happens to be the state of the Jewish people, the suspicion of bigotry must be considered.

5. The BDS movement is immoral because it would hurt the wrong people.

It would hurt Palestinian workers who will lose their jobs if economic sanctions are directed against firms that employ them. It would hurt artists and academics, many of whom are the strongest voices for peace and an end to the occupation. It would hurt those suffering from illnesses all around the world who would be helped by Israeli medicine and the collaboration between Israeli scientists and other scientists. It would hurt the high-tech industry around the world because Israel contributes disproportionally to the development of such life-enhancing technology.

6. The BDS movement is immoral because it would encourage Iran—the world's leading facilitator of international terrorism—to unleash its surrogates, such as Hezbollah and Hamas, against Israel, in the expectation that if Israel were to respond to rocket attacks, the pressure for BDS against Israel would increase, as it did when Israel responded to thousands of rockets from Gaza in 2008 and 2009.

7. The BDS movement is immoral because it focuses the world's attention away from far greater injustices, including genocide.

By focusing disproportionately on Israel, the human rights community pays disproportionately less attention to the other occupations, such as those by China, Russia, and Turkey, and to other humanitarian disasters such as that occurring in Syria.

8. The BDS movement is immoral because it promotes false views regarding the nation-state of the Jewish people, exaggerates its flaws and thereby promotes a new variation on the world's oldest prejudice, namely anti-Semitism.

It is not surprising therefore that the BDS movement is featured on neo-Nazi, Holocaust denial, and other overtly anti-Semitic websites and is promoted by some of the world's most notorious haters, such as David Duke.

9. The BDS movement is immoral because it reflects and encourages a double standard of judgment and response regarding human rights violations.

By demanding more of Israel, the nation-state of the Jewish people, it expects less of other states, people, cultures, and religions, thereby reifying a form of colonial racism and reverse bigotry that hurts the victims of human rights violations inflicted by others.

10. The BDS movement will never achieve its goals.

Neither the Israeli government nor the Israeli people will ever capitulate to the extortionate means implicit in

BDS. They will not and should not make important decisions regarding national security and the safety of their citizens on the basis of immoral threats. Moreover, were Israel to compromise its security in the face of such threats, the result would be more wars, more death, and more suffering.

All decent people who seek peace in the Middle East should join together in opposing the immoral BDS movement. Use your moral voices to demand that both the Israeli government and the Palestinian Authority accept a compromise peace that assures the security of Israel and the fidelity of a peaceful and democratic Palestinian state. The way forward is not by immoral extortionate threats that do more harm than good, but rather by negotiations, compromise, and goodwill.

40

Debate between Alan Dershowitz
and John Dugard

August 14, 2014

O N AUGUST 14, 2014, as the war was winding
down, I debated Professor John Dugard by Skype,
in front of a live audience at the University of
the Witwatersrand, in Johannesburg, South Africa.[1]
Professor Dugard, the former dean of that law school, had
served as chairman and rapporteur of the United Nations
Commissions investigating human rights in Palestine and
had written reports accusing Israel of war crimes. He had
also served as a judge on the United Nations' International
Court of Justice. He is widely regarded as the world's most
distinguished accuser against Israel.

Professor Dershowitz: Thank you. I appreciate the opportunity to present my perspective. I was asked to begin by
adding a historical context of the events in Gaza.

In 1937, the Peel Commission proposed the division
of the British land into a Jewish state and an Arab state.

---

1 Some minor editorial changes have been made from the transcript to correct
typographical errors and grammar and to avoid repetition. There has been
no change in the substance of the debate.

The Jewish agency accepted. The Arab states rejected. In 1947, the UN created its partition. Again, the Jewish agency accepted and a year later declared the State of Israel. The Arabs rejected and all surrounding Arab armies attacked Israel, killing 1 percent of its population, including many Holocaust survivors.

Following the 1967 war, which was caused by Egypt and Syria threatening a genocidal war against Israel, the Israelis offered to return the captured territory in exchange for recognition and peace. All the Arab nations went to Khartoum and issued their three famous noes: "No peace. No recognition. No negotiation."

Then in 2000 to 2001, Ehud Barak and Bill Clinton offered the Palestinians a state on about 95 percent of the West Bank and all of the Gaza Strip, ending the military occupation and the civilian settlements. Yasser Arafat rejected that and began the Intifada in which four thousand people were killed.

In 2008, Prime Minister Ehud Olmert offered an even more generous proposal to the Palestinians, which was never responded to.

Now to Gaza. In 2005 Prime Minister Sharon ended the civilian settlements in Gaza, removed all the settlers, and all the soldiers.

At that time, there was no blockade and it was certainly possible for Gaza to develop itself freely and effectively. Israel maintained some security controls to prevent the import of weapons, but between 2005 and 2007, there was no blockade.

The response was massive numbers of rockets which played Russian roulette with the lives of Israeli children and other civilians. The blockade was—and this is very important—the *result* of the rockets. The rockets are not the result of the blockade.

In 2006, the tunnels were first used to kidnap an Israeli soldier, Gilad Shalit, and kill two other Israeli soldiers and wound four others. That was Israel's first indication that this tunnel warfare was about to commence.

Hamas, at about that time, instead of developing itself independently, developed a brilliant public relations strategy that would involve a double war crime. Their strategy was to fire rockets and build tunnels from the densely populated areas in the Gaza Strip.

If any of you have been to the Gaza Strip as I have, you know that there are many empty areas in Gaza between the major cities, but Hamas elected to put their tunnels and fire their rockets in the most densely populated areas, using civilians as human shields.

Hamas's goal is to induce Israel to fire back in self-defense. The end result is civilian casualties, but I maintain, and I'd like to hear Professor Dugard's response to this, that the civilian casualties under these circumstances are primarily the responsibility of Hamas.

An example from criminal law: If a bank robber robs a bank and takes the teller as a hostage and begins to fire from behind the hostage, and the police in order to prevent the killing of some of the bank customers come in and try their best not to kill the hostage, but in the end do shoot and kill the hostage, who is responsible for that murder? Certainly not the policeman who fired the shot, but rather the person who used the human shield. I think the same is true of Hamas in Gaza.

The question: When you have an enemy that wants to maximize civilian casualties both on its own side and on the Israeli side, how should a democracy respond? What can it do? Surely, I think Professor Dugard would agree that Israel has the right of self-defense. They try to destroy the rocket launchers and they try to destroy the tunnels from which terrorists come and can kill civilians. They have a right to attack such military targets even if the military targets are in densely populated areas, so long as the rules of proportionality are abided by.

The rules of proportionality, though complex, can simply be stated as follows: the military value of the target has to be proportional to the reasonably anticipated civilian casualties. The military targets that Israel attacked—particularly the rocket launchers and the terrorist tunnels—are extremely important military targets.

Indeed Israeli intelligence had reports, just before they went in on the ground to attack the tunnels, that there was a massive attack planned through the tunnels which would have killed many Israeli civilians.

Now, proportionality involves a difficult calculus, and it often has to be made during the fog of war and mistakes are made. The best evidence is that Israel killed a number of its own soldiers in friendly fire episodes.

The tunnels could not be destroyed without ground troops fighting in densely populated areas where Hamas chose to place their entrances. You cannot attack the tunnels from the air, because Israel doesn't know exactly the route of the tunnels. They do know where the entrances are. The entrances are often in mosques, and there is a videotape of that,[2] and near schools.

Israel had to send in troops on the ground knowing, to be sure, that there would not only be some casualties among their own soldiers—more than sixty of them were killed—but also casualties among the civilians that lived in the areas near the tunnel entrances that were selected by Hamas.

2 Ian Deitch and Ibrahim Barzak, "Israel Vows to Destroy Hamas Tunnels, Deaths Spike," *Yahoo News*, 31 July 2014.

I maintain that Israel satisfied the rules of proportionality. They distinguished between military and civilian targets. And they did not engage in collective punishment. Their actions were not intended to be punitive in nature. They were intended to be preventive.

If Hamas had decided to put their tunnels in the open areas and fire their rockets from the open areas, there would have been few if any civilian casualties. In fact, during the Six-Day War, there were very few civilian casualties.

That's my case for Israel's actions in Gaza. Now, let's turn to the future. If Israel were to be improperly condemned for its self-defense actions, as it was by the *Goldstone Report*, this will only encourage Hamas to continue to operate its dead civilian strategy because that strategy works.

Israel wins militarily on the ground, but always loses in the court of public opinion, because it's far easier for the media to show dead children and dead women than it is to show the context.

In fact, Hamas refuses to allow journalists to photograph rockets being fired or photograph the entrances of the tunnels in densely civilian areas. All the public sees are the results, the dead children. To go back to my analogy, all they see are the policemen shooting the hostage. They don't see the bank robber who held the hostage and caused his death.

What should happen now is that Gaza should be demilitarized. The blockade should end, with exceptions for military rockets and equipment necessary to build tunnels, and Israel and Palestinian authority should engage in peace talks toward a two-state solution on the West Bank.

If the Gaza Strip is then controlled by the Palestinian Authority, there could be a complete two-state solution. Israel should negotiate with, but it shouldn't recognize or legitimate an organization like Hamas, which is really no different from ISIS.

Just yesterday Hamas claimed credit for the murder of three Israelis including one American citizen. You cannot legitimate an organization that engages in kidnapping and murder. Thank you very much.

Professor Dugard: Let me begin by thanking you for inviting me. Just two preliminary points; I'm not going to comment on the history. That is the agreement, Professor Dershowitz's portrayal of the history. Secondly I'm going to avoid the use of the term "terrorism" or "terrorist" because both sides accuse each other of being terrorists.

Before I start, I think it's important we have the facts on the table because they do inform the debate. To date, two thousand Palestinians have been killed and ten thousand wounded. Sixty-seven Israelis have been killed, of whom three are civilians. Professor Dershowitz said, and I would agree with him, that Israel acted in self-defense, but quite frankly I do not.

I know that Israel argues that it acts in self-defense and President Obama had supported this and both houses of Congress had supported this unanimously. It's the only thing those two houses can agree upon, but I think it's important to stress that Gaza is occupied territory. It has been occupied for forty-seven years.

The test for occupation is effective control, and Israel is in effective control of Gaza. It controls the land crossings, the sea space, the air space, and it has regular incursions into Gaza, so it does have effective control over the territory.

Israel disputes this. It argues that it is simply a hostile entity in terms of international law, but the general view is that it is occupied territory.

Now, once you accept it is an occupied territory, it's quite clear that Israel's purpose is not to act in self-defense, but to punish occupied people. In other words, it acts not as victims as in fact it portrays itself but rather as policemen.

I think you seem to look at it in the context of the French Resistance in the Second World War. If the French Resistance had fired rockets into Germany during the Second World War, you wouldn't have [criticized] it.

In the very nature of occupation, people are going to resist. From time immemorial, occupied people have resisted occupation. They have fought back and they will continue to do so whether Israel likes it or not.

Israel and Hamas must comply with the two cardinal principles of humanitarian law. They must observe the principal of distinction, which means that they should distinguish between civilian targets and military targets in firing rockets and bombarding each other.

Secondly, there is the principle of proportionality, which means that excessive force should not be used in the attack.

Now, I'm prepared to accept that Hamas is guilty of war crimes in the sense that it has fired rockets indiscriminately into civilian areas, but of course it has been rather ineffective in this respect because only three Israeli civilians have been killed.

Israel on the other hand has engaged in both indiscriminate firing of rockets and shots into Gaza, and it has done so by using force excessively. Over two thousand people have been killed. Ten thousand injured. There has been extensive damage to property and the whole Gaza community has been terrorized.

Today, I received news that the parents of a friend of mine from Gaza had been killed, so this does make one aware of the fact that it is a killing field. Schools have been destroyed. Rockets have been fired at mosques and at hospitals, and there are also serious allegations of executions [by the IDF] of Palestinians.

I carried out an investigation into Gaza in 2009. We had the same allegations from people who had been carrying white flags and consequently shot by members of the IDF.

Currently Israel's defense, which has been eloquently put forward by Professor Dershowitz, [is] namely that Hamas uses human shields, that it places its rocket launchers in urban areas and not in rural areas. Obviously, it could place its rocket launchers in rural areas; it would be easy targets for Israel and its drones.

It places its rocket launchers in [urban] areas, but whether it does so in a way which exposes the civilian population is not clear. There is no evidence that it does so, and that's a matter of fact which must be determined by an international judicial tribunal.

As far as tunnels are concerned, it seems that the tunnels are used to attack military targets. Recently, there was a debate on an Israeli website in which an Israeli made it quite clear that the tunnels did not lead to the kibbutz as Prime Minister Netanyahu has stated, but rather they led to military targets. Certainly to date, the tunnels have been used only for military targets such as the capture of Gilad Shalit and the killing of IDF members.

These are questions of fact, and facts must be determined by an international court; if not by the International Criminal Court, then by a special tribunal. I'm told that Israel has been taking photographs of its activities in the Gaza Strip, so presumably it has evidence and there's no reason why it should not present them to an international tribunal.

I would say Israel is guilty of committing war crimes. I also believe that it is guilty of committing crimes against humanity, because it meets all the requirements for crimes against humanity.

Some argue that it meets the requirements for the crime

of all crimes, genocide. On the face of it, there's nothing to substantiate this predicate. My own view is that one should not infer, especially intent to commit genocide, which is required for the crime of genocide, from outrageous genocidal statements in the Israeli Knesset, parliament, or by the number of persons killed. When you look to what I think is the real purpose of Israel's action, and that is to collectively punish the people of Gaza, to terrorize every day, and punish them.

This is in violation of the fourth Geneva Convention. It's done so previously by collective punishment, and it is adventurous by shooting and bombarding Gaza. In my view, there's a prima facie case against Israel, that it has committed war crimes, and crimes against humanity.

Can we now briefly turn to the future?

If necessary, international monitors should be employed to monitor this siege, monitor the crossings from both Rafah and [other] areas into Gaza. Secondly, I feel it's very important that there should be direct talks between Israel and Hamas, and United States and Hamas. I find it ridiculous that the United States is prepared to talk to Taliban in Afghanistan, but not prepared to talk to Hamas, and that's only because the Israeli government disapproves of direct talks.

Finally, there can be no peace without justice. That means that there must be accountability for those who have committed international crimes, both in Hamas and the Islamic Jihad, and in the Israeli government, and the IDF.

I cannot understand why Israel—if it has all this evidence, it claims to be innocent—[why] it is not prepared to further the matter to the International Criminal Court, or to suggest that an international ad hoc tribunal be set up to hear the case.

Instead, Israel and the United States have pressured the

International Criminal Court into refusing to get into this conversation.

I conclude by saying that accountability is of great importance in this country. Thank you.

Professor Dershowitz: The implications of Professor Dugard's position are very dangerous. First, you give Israel no credit for ending the settlements, and ending the military presence in the Gaza Strip. That makes it much harder for Israel to accept a two-state solution on the West Bank, where rockets could close its airport and endanger all of its population.

Second, he makes the very questionable statement that a people under occupation are entitled to kill civilians with impunity, and that Israel has no right to self-defense. That it can't defend its children against the Russian roulette of rockets being fired at its schools and school buses. My God, what kind of world would we live in if they couldn't engage in such self-defense?

I was in one of those tunnels. The tunnel I was in six weeks ago exited yards away from a kibbutz kindergarten with fifty-seven children in it. My challenge to you, Professor Dugard, is are you actually suggesting that Israel had no legal way [of] stopping those tunnels, but that it simply had to wait for terrorists to come out, and risk killing 57, or 570, or 5,700 children? Is that your definition of international law?

What would South Africa do if there were tunnels dug under it from Zimbabwe, if rockets were being fired? Would it simply say, "No, we're not going to do anything"? Does the fact that some people think that there's a continued occupation, even though there was no military presence, deny Israel the most fundamental right of self-defense?

Professor Dugard: I accept that Israel has the right to destroy tunnels that are being employed, not against civilians, but against its military. I accept that it is entitled to destroy the tunnels, but it does so not in self-defense, but as a policeman that is enforcing the occupation, that is suppressing a vote by an occupied people. I think that is where we differ fundamentally.

Secondly, as far as my failure to give credit to Israel for withdrawing from Gaza is concerned, I think it's important to stress that Israel simply could not cope with the presence of the IDF in Gaza before 2005. Because there were small numbers of settlers in the territory.

There had to be a tremendous IDF presence in order to protect the settlers. Hopeless, but pretty strategically, and economically, impossible to continue occupying Gaza on the ground.

The fact that it has withdrawn its troops from permanent occupation does not undermine the fact that it remains in effective control by other means and that it is therefore an occupying power, and it is simply suppressing people who vote from a rebellious occupied people.

AUDIENCE QUESTIONS

Male Audience Member: Israeli authorities have confirmed that no tunnel actually exits closer than two miles from any Israeli civilian population center. Question to Professor Dugard in particular, what are the limits of legitimate resistance against occupation? What is allowed, what is not allowed, from a military and civilian resistance point of view?

Professor Dugard: As I said in my presentation, an occupied people is entitled to resist the occupation. History says that this has always been done, and occupied people will continue to resist occupation.

One must bear in mind that in the same way Israel is subject to the rules of the international humanitarian law, so too is the occupied people. It is bound to refrain from firing rockets indiscriminately into civilian areas, however ineffective it may be.

There may be a right to resist, but it is subject to the rules of international humanitarianism.

Professor Dershowitz: First, let me correct a categorically false statement that was made by the questioner, namely that no tunnel exits are closer than two miles away from Israeli population centers.

The statement can't be true, because Israel doesn't know where the exits are. The exits are still secret. They only know where the entrances are. But several tunnels that they have discovered have exits that are much, much closer to civilian areas.

The one I was in was merely yards away from a kibbutz, which is a population center. It may not be a city, but it was far less than two miles away from cities and towns, so that's just a categorically false statement.

It's those kinds of statements that are repeated in the media over and over again, and repeated at events like this. Second, even Professor Dugard concedes that [Hamas] is not allowed to fire rockets. That automatically gives Israel the right of self-defense against those rockets, and they can't build tunnels to go into Israel to kill Israelis.

Israel has the right to self-defense. You want to call it a police action, want to call it self-defense, it makes absolutely no difference. The only way Israel can stop the tunnels, which Professor Dugard acknowledges they have a right to do, is to send in ground troops.

They tried desperately to minimize civilian casualties by giving warnings, by knocking on the roof, by making phone calls, but because Hamas put these tunnels in mosques, in schools, in very densely surrounded areas, in order to avoid them being caught by Israelis. Professor Dugard is right. If they were put in the open fields, then Israel would attack them. But that's what the law requires. It doesn't allow you to put them in densely populated areas in order to avoid attack militarily.

Israel had the right to destroy the tunnels, and again I challenge Professor Dugard, what would you have done if the only way of closing the tunnels was by sending in ground troops? Would you send in ground troops? Professor Dugard, please answer my direct question.

Professor Dugard: The question as I understand it was, there was an admission by the Israeli government apparently, that there were no tunnel exits sufficiently near civilian parts.

Professor Dershowitz: It's a totally false statement. It's a lie. No Israeli official has ever said that. None of the tunnels have exits within two miles of any civilian population. I will donate money to your favorite charity if you can find a statement by an Israeli official that says that none of the tunnels exits are within two miles of any civilian populations. It's false. It's just false, I'm sorry.[3]

Professor Dugard: There was a debate on this matter. There, Israelis stated very clearly that no tunnel exited close to

---

3 Hana Levi Julian, "IDF Kills Swarms of Terrorists Emerging from Tunnels near 2 Kibbutzim," *The Jewish Press*, 21 July 2014.

[civilian areas]. It is a question of fact, and I think this should be referred to international tribunal.

Secondly, as far as how Israel should proceed, it should proceed to close the tunnels, but it should not in the process indiscriminately kill civilians, and Israel has deliberately, I believe, targeted hospitals, schools, and mosques, and civilian homes.

It has shown no regard for human life. It has behaved in a callous, disgusting manner. I've carried out an investigation of operations across maybe 2009. I was appalled by the level of destructions that I saw, and by the stories that I heard of coldblooded executions carried out by members of the IDF.

I don't think that one should disregard the fact that the Israeli forces have not complied with the laws of war, and they have committed war crimes.

Professor Dershowitz: That's your opinion, and that's not based on fact at all. I recommended in an article I wrote, that there should be an ad hoc investigation both of Hamas, and of Israel, but it shouldn't be done from the UN Council on Human Rights, which is biased, and it shouldn't be chaired by somebody who before hearing any evidence has already said, "Netanyahu ought to be put in the dock, and brought before the International Criminal Court."

It should be chaired by somebody like Luis Ocampo, who was the first prosecutor of the International Criminal Court. Objective people who have stated no positions, not Professor Dugard, not myself, but people who have never stated any positions on this. Not people who have already shown a bias.

If any Israeli soldier ever engaged in a cold-blooded murder, he'd be court-martialed. He'd be brought in front of a court.[4] Some have been disciplined, but in every army there are bad apples. You don't judge a country by what his worst soldier does, you judge a country by how it responds to what its worst soldier does.

In Hamas's case, they glorify and name parks after murderers of children, after the Vogel family murderers, that killed a group of people in their beds. Was that legitimate self-defense? Is that legitimate opposition to an occupation? No. Israel, according to Colonel Kemp, a British military expert [who] said, "No country in history has ever shown more concern for civilians, and has ever done more to avoid civilian casualties, than Israel."

Israel has done better than my own country, done better than England, done better than NATO. Of course it's made mistakes, but the idea of using words like "genocide" and words like "war crimes" is just outrageous, and shows a particular bias against the nation-state of the Jewish people.

Professor Dugard: Dershowitz supports Luis Moreno Ocampo as a judge, and he was a prosecutor of the ICC. I cannot understand why both Israel and the United States so vehemently oppose International Criminal Court for this matter.

Professor Dershowitz: Three good reasons. Number one, Palestine has to earn its right to be declared a state, and to be recognized by the International Criminal Court as an actual

---

4 "Chief Military Prosecutor Dani Efroni has ordered the Israeli Defense Forces' investigative police unit to open 99 investigations into the army's operation in the Gaza Strip over the summer...." Gill Cohen, "IDF to Open Criminal Probes into 5 Gaza War Cases," *Haaretz*, 10 September 2014. Needless to say, neither Hamas nor the Palestinian Authority has opened any probes into Hamas war crimes.

state. The United Nations can't do that through its General Assembly.

Number two, if it were brought before the International Criminal Court, Israel would be found to have a completely legitimate legal system, and complementarity would deny jurisdiction to the Criminal Court.

Third of all, I think Israel would be vindicated by any fair and objective evaluation, but it was taken before the International Court of Justice—which is not international, it's not a court, and it knows nothing about justice—Israel has never served on the Court of Justice. When it decided the security barrier case, it barely mentioned the fact that the security barrier had prevented thousands of acts of terrorism. If you're prepared to present a fair court, I am prepared certainly to recommend to Israel that it have a fair hearing in front of a fair court.

But to be indicted based on the kinds of speculation that you just set out, of course not. Nobody would ever agree to be put in the dock for engaging in an act of self-defense.

I would say that the International Court of Justice is to justice for Israel what Southern courts were, headed by Klan members, in relation to justice for blacks in the South. Or what apartheid courts were in South Africa in relation to a black defendant.

Israel cannot, under any circumstances, expect to receive justice by that disgraceful institution, run by the United Nations, which has shown its bias and bigotry against Israel for many years.

The United Nations has condemned Israel more often than they have Iran, Cambodia. Even during the Cambodian killings, where three to five million people were killed, there was not one condemnation by the UN, but that was the same year that the UN voted that Zionism was a form of racism.

How do you expect Israel to receive justice in front of what is essentially an apartheid court?

I think people in South Africa should realize that there was no justice in South Africa prior to Mandela's release from prison, and there is no justice in United Nations courts when it comes to Israel.

Professor Dugard: The International Criminal Court is not the United Nations Court. Would you be prepared to submit the matter to the International Criminal Court? If so, why does Israel and the United States resist it so strongly?

Professor Dershowitz: First of all, the United States is not a member of the International Criminal Court, and Israel is not a member of the International Criminal Court, and for very, very good reasons. The International Criminal Court has not yet proved its credibility to do objective justice.

I was invited to speak to the International Criminal Court a few years ago, when prosecutor Ocampo was there, and although he himself was extremely fair and unbiased, I found many staff members had very predisposed views regarding the United States, Israel, and the West in general.

I would accept an ad hoc commission, headed by Luis Ocampo, with its members to be picked by people like Luis Ocampo, without anybody who's ever expressed any view regarding the Middle East conflict, international scholars of renown, with an equal claim against Hamas and against Israel.

Let them look at the facts and decide whether Hamas has committed double war crimes, whether Israel has acted in self-defense, whether Israel has satisfied the rules of proportionality, distinction, and opposition to collective punishment.

I am confident that any fair court would convict Hamas, and acquit Israel.

Male Audience Member: My question simply is do you continue to entertain that acts of ethnic cleansing were not committed in the process of the emergence of the State of Israel?

Professor Dershowitz: No country in modern history has ever been established in a more lawful manner. Starting with the Balfour Declaration, the Peel Commission Report, the UN Declarations, the League of Nations Declarations, Israel was established in 1948 absolutely lawfully.

It was then attacked by all the Arab countries. Had it not been attacked, the Arab population would have remained exactly where it was. There would have been no refugee problem. The Arabs attacked and told their people, leave and they would come back victorious. About seven hundred thousand or eight hundred thousand left.

Some under pressure, some voluntarily, some people were going to come back victoriously.

At the same time about eight hundred thousand Jews were expelled from Arab countries. From Iraq, from North Africa, there was essentially an exchange in population. No, there was no ethnic cleansing at all.

As far as the negotiation posture, just ask Bill Clinton, or Hillary Clinton. They both recently made statements saying that it was absolutely Yasser Arafat who turned down the opportunity for a two-state solution.

If not for Yasser Arafat's untimely death—I say untimely because had he died four years earlier, we would today be celebrating the fourteenth anniversary of Palestinian statehood. He was given an enormous opportunity to help his people.

The prince of Saudi Arabia said he committed a crime against the Palestinian people by not accepting the offer at Camp David and Taba by Clinton and Barack. Not only do I stand by my position, but I reiterate it.

You want to see the documentation in support of it, I have it in the five books I've written about this subject with documentary proof that Israel did not engage in any kind of ethnic cleansing. Look, you can find historians in any country that will dispute historical accounts.

You can find historians in South Africa that would dispute accounts that Nelson Mandela has made. The question is not what do individual historians say, but what the truth is.

You are challenging Israel's legitimacy as the nation of Jewish people, you're shaking your head saying yes, and that is a nonstarter. Israel is not going away.

Israel is as legitimate as South Africa, as legitimate as the United States of America, as legitimate as New Zealand, which did ethnically cleanse its population, or Australia, which did ethnically cleanse its population.

Israel is here to stay, no matter how much you shake your head.

Professor Dugard: First of all, I think the historians convincingly [demonstrate] that there was Israeli cleansing, so I think the historical record is very clear on that. Secondly, as far as Israel's own system of justice is concerned, Professor Dershowitz had suggested that the principle of complementarity would prevent the International Criminal Court from hearing any dispute.

Israel has no [good] record when it comes to prosecuting crimes committed by the IDF. Take, for instance, the events after the 2008–2009 Operation Cast Lead. Several reports showed convincingly that Israel had committed international crimes.

They identified the victims and the assailants, but all Israel did was to prosecute someone for theft of a credit card from the Palestinian. There was no prosecution whatsoever for real crimes. That was a disgraceful example of Israeli justice.

I would like to just comment on the question of occupation. I think it's very clear that Israel is not only in occupation of Gaza, but it's in illegal occupation of Gaza, because it refuses to carry out its obligations.

Who is responsible for funding projects in this occupied territory of Gaza? Its foreign donors. Israel has withdrawn its financial involvement and has completely ignored its own responsibility for taking care of an occupied territory.

Instead, it has imposed and sieged upon Gaza, which has left Gaza completely without most basic commodities. I think one must understand that Hamas's resistance to the siege is the primary reason for this conflict.

Also I'd like to stress that Israel was largely responsible for starting this conflict. You would recall that following the death of three Israeli teenagers, Israel embarked upon a savage suppression of Hamas in the West Bank.

There was no evidence that Hamas was responsible for those killings. Israel started the suppression of Hamas in the West Bank, and that sparked off the rocket firing from Gaza. I don't think it's clear, or it's fair to say, that Hamas was responsible for initiating the present conflict.

Professor Dershowitz: Hamas leaders admitted responsibility for this yesterday.

Professor Dugard: I was not aware of that.

Male Audience Member: If it wasn't for the Iron Dome, I

think there would be a lot more casualties on the Israeli end as well.

My question is, I understand the principle of distinction, and it's required to distinguish between a military objective and a population, and to direct operations against only military objectives.

Military objectives include combatants, which by their nature, location, and purpose, make effective contributions to military action. My question is that if there are rockets being fired out of schools, and being fired out of mosques, and being fired out of hospitals, for the principle of distinction, wouldn't these be considered military objectives?

Professor Dugard: If we have evidence that mosques and schools are being used for rocket launching, then Israel will be entitled to respond, but there is no clear evidence... We find no evidence to support Israel's case. I suspect that this time around, there is still no evidence to support it.

These are matters that should be referred to international tribunal for investigation. I stand by my view that Israel has acted without regard for civilian lives and accounts for the high number of civilian deaths in the Gaza Strip.

Professor Dershowitz: What accounts for the high number of civilian deaths in the Gaza Strip is that Hamas adamantly refuses to allow civilians to use the shelters that it built. It only allows its terrorists, yes, I'm using the word terrorists.

Terrorists are people who target civilians, children and women like the Vogel family, and like the three children who were kidnapped. They are terrorists, yes, they are terrorists. Hamas doesn't allow its civilians to use the shelters, only the terrorists can use the shelters.

They want civilians to die, they want them to be killed. Professor Dugard, you can go over the evidence in mosques, look online. There is a videotape of a tunnel being built from a prayer room in a mosque. There is a videotape on Indian television and French television of rockets being fired from near UN facilities.[5]

If you acknowledge that a mosque that is used to fire rockets is a legitimate military target, then Israel cannot be charged with any violation if it is firing back on targets and abiding by the rules of proportionality, which it is.

What people are afraid of are judges like you, Professor Dugard. I would not want Israel to be tried in front of you. You've made up your mind. You said you saw the evidence. Hamas didn't let you see the evidence. The only reason they let you in to look at the evidence is they know which side you are on.

If an objective person like Ocampo came in, they would hide the evidence from him.

Female Audience Member: Professor Dershowitz, you've openly and publicly supported practices such as waterboarding, in other words, torture, in the United States—

Professor Dershowitz: Absolute lie. I have opposed waterboarding—

Female Audience Member: Can I finish my question? As far as I understand, as far as I've read, you support, under certain circumstances, the use of waterboarding by the US administration in the case of terrorism. To me, this indicates that you do not respect the fact that there are certain boundaries that cannot be crossed, in international relations, in terms of human dignity.

---

5 See footage from NDTV (http://www.ndtv.com/video/player/news/watch-ndtv-exclusive-how-hamas-assembles-and-fires-rockets/332910) and France 24 (https://www.youtube.com/watch?v=pGOUXS7KPNI).

Professor Dershowitz: You have absolutely and categorically lied to this audience. I am opposed to waterboarding. I have led the campaign against torture and waterboarding in the United States. I have been opposed to all forms of torture from the very beginning.

I don't know what you are reading or what you're seeing, but the statement in fact you made is categorically and unequivocally false. What I have argued is that if there is going to be any use of these despicable tactics, there should be at least a warrant requirement before their use. That's my position. Please don't misrepresent it.

Professor Dugard: [Dershowitz] has repeatedly praised Luis Moreno Ocampo, the former prosecutor of the International Criminal Court. It's important to realize that Ocampo took three years to consider the 2009 Palestinian Declaration accepting the jurisdiction as a court.

He could have taken the decision on this matter within one month, if he was going to reach the conclusion that he reached. I really believe he was put under tremendous pressure from the United States, as I believe the present prosecutor is.

One should not underestimate the influence of the United States in the International Criminal Court, and the decision to prosecute. I believe that the present prosecutor could prosecute on the basis of the 2009 declaration, but under pressure from the United States, and under pressure from Israel—

Professor Dershowitz: What you are saying is that the International Criminal Court is subject to pressure, political pressure, and that it is not really a legitimate court?

Male Audience Member: Professor Dugard, your entire argument is predicated on, based on the blockade or the circle blockade by the Israelis in Gaza, but you selectively ignored the fact that between period of 2005 and 2007, there was no blockade whatsoever.

In fact, the blockade only came following the indiscriminate rockets which are being fired from Gaza into the civilian population of Israel. Only thereafter, then Israel, in your own words, becomes a policeman to effectively monitor, or it attempts to monitor, or stop the rockets that were coming indiscriminately during the period which there was no blockade. Can you please answer that?

Professor Dugard: It's important to stress that the blockade has been imposed as a punishment upon the entire population of Gaza, that Israel has made no effort to distinguish between its punishment of Hamas and its punishment of the people of Gaza. That's why I say that it has engaged in an unlawful siege of Gaza. Its occupation is unlawful.

It's important to end on the note that I started on. That is that Israel has engaged in indiscriminate firing at and shooting of civilian targets, and this is evidenced very clearly by the number of Palestinian deaths and the number of wounded people and the extensive damage to property in the Gaza Strip.

I don't think that one can in any way justify Israel's action. The international community, public opinion, and the world outside the United States and Israel is rightly outraged by Israel's behavior. I do hope that Israel has the opportunity to appear before a proper International Criminal Court. I'm convinced it would be found guilty of war crimes and crimes against humanity.

Professor Dershowitz: The very fact that international opinion is against Israel when Israel has been engaging in an act of self-defense against Hamas, that uses human shields and fires indiscriminately and uses tunnels of death, is part of the problem.

The very fact that public opinion is against Israel as the result of statements made by Professor Dugard and others, is why Hamas is going to continue to do this. Why Hamas is going to continue to engage in terrorism. Why it's going to continue to kidnap young children and murder them! Why it's going to continue to be like ISIS except that its charter is somewhat worse.

The very fact that Professor Dugard won't recognize matters of degree, that Israel did a good thing when it ended its military occupation of Gaza and took its civilian settlements out of Gaza, that he refuses to give any credit for that makes it difficult for Israel to do the same thing on the West Bank.

Israel cannot completely end military control over its borders. It can never allow tunnels to be dug under its borders.

I say this categorically, no country in the history of the world faced with threats comparable to those faced by Israel has ever complied better with the rule of law, has ever done more to protect civilians, and has ever done more to protect human rights and human liberty.

Nor has any government faced with such threats ever had a better judiciary that has held its soldiers accountable. I challenge you all in the audience to think of any country faced with comparable threats that has done better than Israel. If I am right, then why, I ask you, is Israel singled out for this double standard?

Why, among all the people in the world that are committing horrendous crimes, is Israel the only country that is now suggested to be brought to the court of public opinion and to the courts of law? Answer that question, please.

How to Assure Another Gaza War in Two Years

EVEN IF THE CEASE-FIRE between Israel and Hamas holds for a while, it will probably not last.[1] The international community is doing everything in its power to assure that once Hamas regroups and rearms, it will once again attack Israel with better rockets, deeper tunnels and more effective use of human shields. Hamas will once again deploy its dead baby strategy—placing its rocket launchers and tunnel entrances in densely populated areas so that Israel will have to kill civilians in order to attack these military targets. It will reprise this strategy because it always works. It works because Hamas makes it easy for the media to show the dead civilians but difficult to show the rockets and tunnels behind and beneath these civilian human shields.

---

1 Although I have long advocated, and continue to advocate, a two-state solution based roughly on the parameters outlined in the 2000–2001 Barak-Clinton proposals, and the 2008 offer by Ehud Olmert, I seriously doubt that any such resolution would solve the Gaza problem or would end the battle with Hamas, which continues to believe, and act on the belief, that the only solution is the destruction of Israel through terrorism.

The result of this one-sided emotional display of dead bodies is outrage against Israel for causing so many civilians deaths and demands for international investigations and prosecutions of Israeli officials and soldiers. Israel wins the war on the ground, while Hamas wins the war of international public opinion. Hamas then regroups and rearms, while Israel suffers permanent reputational damage for doing what every democracy would do—and doing it with fewer civilian casualties. So why shouldn't Hamas repeat its winning tactic over and over again?

One answer might be that Hamas knows that if it once again fires rockets and builds tunnels in densely populated areas, more civilians will die, more buildings will be destroyed, and more misery will be spread among the people of Gaza. Most armies would be deterred by such knowledge. But not Hamas. Not only do its leaders *not* worry about these tragic results, they welcome them. The more dead civilians, the better for implementing their public relations strategy. It worked before and it will work again. So why not repeat it?

The *Goldstone Report*, which blamed Israel for the civilian casualties of Operation Cast Lead in 2008 and 2009, begat the rocket and tunnel attacks that led Israel to conduct Operation Protective Edge. Now Hamas is seeking a sequel to Goldstone—this time conducted by an anti-Israel zealot, who has already convicted Israel and Prime Minister Netanyahu of war crimes before seeing any of the evidence. Sequels beget sequels, and it is entirely predictable that Hamas will win this postwar battle of words and condemnation and that it will try to reprise its victory by once again deploying its reliable dead baby strategy—perhaps in a year, or maybe two, but it will happen. You can count on it.

Indeed on September 7, 2014—just two weeks after Hamas purported to accept the cease-fire—*Haaretz* reported that "Israel has received intelligence indicating that Hamas has begun reconstructing the attack tunnels" and "preparing for the next confrontation with Israel and is focused on replenishing its arsenals [including] M75 rockets capable of reaching... central Israel."[2] The *Jerusalem Post* reported that the official said that "just as Hamas prepared itself following Operation Pillar of Defense in 2012, 'step by step' for the next round, they are already starting to do the same thing now."[3]

The only way to end this recurrent war with far too many casualties is to expose and condemn Hamas's dead baby strategy and to recognize it for the despicable double war crime that it clearly is. Blaming Israel only incentivizes Hamas to fight, pause, fight, pause, and fight again.

So here is the twelve-step program that guarantees a repeat of Hamas's attacks against Israel from behind Palestinian human shields, many of whom will die:

1.   Blame Israel, rather than Hamas, for the dead babies.

2.   Accuse Israel of committing war crimes.

3.   Have the United Nations manufacture evidence and draw mendacious conclusions against Israel.

4.   Have the International Criminal Court open an investigation against Israel.

---

2 Barak Ravid, "Israeli official: Hamas has begun repairing Gaza tunnels," *Haaretz*, September 7, 2014.

3 Herb Keinon, "Hamas already rearming, preparing for next round of fighting with Israel," *The Jerusalem Post*, 7 September 2014. These reports have been disputed by other officials: Amos Harel, "As Gaza Rebuilding Lags, Risk of Renewed War Grows," *Haaretz*, 10 September 2014.

5. Call for divestment, boycotts, and sanctions against Israel.

6. Demand that the United States cut off aid to Israel.

7. Have "academics" offer opinions that it is lawful for people under occupation to resist by firing rockets from civilian areas at civilian targets and digging tunnels whose entrances and exits are in civilian areas.

8. Have Holocaust survivors and their children place ads in newspapers comparing what Israel does in self-defense to the Nazi genocide of Jews, without even mentioning the threat to Israel posed by the rockets and tunnels. (See ad in the *New York Times*, August 23, 2014, p. A13)

9. Uncritically accept at face value the Hamas-approved statistics regarding alleged civilian deaths among Palestinian civilians, despite Hamas's long history of doctoring these numbers.

10. Focus on the comparative number of Palestinian and Israeli deaths, without explaining that it is part of the Hamas strategy to increase the number of Palestinian deaths by using civilians as human shields and reserving the shelters only for terrorists.

11. Have Nobel Peace Prize winners such as Jimmy Carter and Desmond Tutu condemn Israel for using "disproportionate force."

12. Treat democratic Israel as morally comparable to, or worse than, terrorist Hamas.

Here, in contrast, is the two-step program for reducing the likelihood that Hamas will again fire rockets and employ terrorist tunnels against Israeli civilians from Palestinian civilian areas:

1. Condemn Hamas for starting the war, for firing at civilians from civilian areas, and for deliberately trying to increase the number of civilian deaths by reserving their shelters for terrorists and not for civilians.

2. Disarm Hamas and don't allow it to rearm.[4]

The problem is that the international community seems to be following the twelve-step rather than the two-step program. So, unless things change, stay tuned for a replay of the current tragedy.

4 On September 10, 2014, President Obama delivered a major speech outlining the proposed military campaign against ISIS. He said that the US "will hunt down terrorists who threaten our country, wherever they are." He continued: "If you threaten America, you will find no safe haven." (Mark Landler, "Obama Promises Sustained Effort to Rout Militants," the *New York Times*, September 11, 2014, p. A1.) This is precisely the approach Israel has taken against terrorists who threaten the nation-state of the Jewish people. Yet many of those who support US action condemn Israel when it seeks to protect its citizens from terrorism.